TEN SENTENCES TO
REVOLUTIONIZE
YOUR  MINISTRY

*SIMPLE TRUTHS THAT
CAN CHANGE EVERYTHING
IN YOUR KIDMIN*

RYAN FRANK

Ten Sentences to Revolutionize Your Ministry: Simple Truths That Can Change Everything in Your Kidmin

by Ryan Frank

copyright ©2018 Ryan Frank

ISBN: 978-1-943294-81-7

Cover design by Martijn van Tilborgh

Pulse is also available on Amazon Kindle, Barnes & Noble Nook and Apple iBooks.

Published by KidzMatter

TABLE OF CONTENTS

DEDICATION

This book is dedicated to all the leaders who called out the best in me. You pushed me to ask the right questions, encouraged me to lean on the Lord, you led me, and you showed me the way. Thank you for believing in me and making investments in my life. I promise to pass it on the next generation of ministry leaders.

INTRODUCTION

HEY, FRIENDS, IT'S RYAN FRANK. Welcome to "10 Sentences to Revolutionize Your Ministry." Thank you for taking this journey with me. I'm excited to jump into 10 game-changing sentences that can forever impact the way you minister to kids and families. You're going to find 10 chapters where we address the nuts and bolts of ministry and how a simple reliance on the Lord in each of these areas could mean all of the difference.

I have the great privilege and opportunity of not only being a pastor, but coming alongside of literally thousands of pastors and ministry leaders, whether it's through one of our books, our magazine, our training programs, or events. Let me tell you something I hear from pastors all the time: "Ryan, I feel stuck."

Do you ever feel stuck in ministry? You're thinking, My pastor just doesn't get it. The board doesn't get it. My youth pastor won't cooperate. I can't deal with those parents one more week. There's always "that kid." You just feel stuck. Maybe you're trying to do new ministry models in an old system. Maybe you're brand new and don't know where to go or who to turn to. Maybe you've been at it for years and you feel like you've become complacent or too comfortable.

The good news is this: you can't always change your circumstances, but you can constantly grow and change. I can't control the people around me or what happens around me, but I can control my ability and my willingness to grow and become a better ministry leader.

Here's a simple reality I want you to understand as we begin this course: growing ministries are led by growing leaders. If you want your ministry to grow (and who doesn't really want their ministry to grow?), you must choose to grow as a leader. You must have a growth mindset.

There are four things that happen when you choose not to grow and change.

First, you get discouraged. It's so easy to lose heart in children's ministry. After all, you're working with all of these volunteers, and you have all of these positions that you need to fill. And you have such a wide panoramic view of the different kinds of kids and families and programs and all the demands and responsibilities that you often feel unappreciated, under-resourced, and understaffed. When you choose not to grow and change, it's easy to become discouraged.

Second, when you choose not to grow and change, you feel alone. It's sad that pastors are some of the most popular yet most lonely people. It's lonely as a ministry leader at times, isn't it? Why is that? Because ministry is taxing. I tell people that salvation is free, but ministry is expensive. When you get serious about doing ministry, it costs you. And if you don't invest in yourself spiritually, you are going to find yourself feeling alone.

Third, when you choose not to grow and change, you burn out. This often happens when we love the ministry of the Lord more than we love the Lord of the ministry. We get so busy working that we don't realize we're burned out until it's happened. No one can derail you any faster than you, and no one can ensure your success any faster than you.

Burnout is not biblical. God never intended for you to burn out. In fact, if you study the Bible, burnout isn't in there. Now, there are people in the Bible who burned up, but there are very few who burned out. By reading this book and applying what's in it, I believe you can avoid burnout.

Finally, when you choose not to grow and change, you become ineffective. Ministry growth is contingent upon your growth. So, you have to choose to grow as a leader. You have to choose to work on your ministry, not just work in your ministry. Being an effective ministry leader requires the commitment to growth and change.

Let me encourage you to take time to invest in yourself. As you read, don't just think about your pastor. Don't just think about those you serve with. Think about yourself, and think about how this can help you as a ministry leader.

Sometimes we pay so much attention to what is seen that we don't pay enough attention to what is happening below the surface. It's so important that you not only give attention to your people and your programs and your pastor, but that you also give attention to yourself. Invest in yourself.

Ministry is all about deposits and withdrawals. If I withdraw too much out of my checking account and I never deposit anything, I'm going to be in trouble, aren't I? In ministry, we give of ourselves constantly. But we must be committed to making deposits into our lives personally, professionally, and spiritually.

A lot of leaders are starving bakers. Do you know what a starving baker is? I heard someone say that you never want to eat from a skinny chef or a starving baker. When a chef is carrying a little weight, what does that tell you? That they like to eat their own food, right? As ministry leaders, we can be starving bakers or skinny chefs. We make food, we deliver food, and we help people, but we aren't eating ourselves. We're starving bakers.

I trust that in this book, you will be challenged to invest in yourself; to start eating, to start exercising, and to make deposits in your life so you can be the leader God wants you to be.

I've titled this course "10 Sentences to Revolutionize Your Ministry." Every sentence begins with this phrase: "Lord, help me..." Why did I choose that phrase? In Matthew 15, we read about the faith of a Canaanite woman. One day Jesus was going through town and a Canaanite woman went up to him to Him and asked for his help. Her daughter was troubled and demon possessed and others had shooed her away. She didn't know what to say except for three very important words. They can be found in Matthew 15:25. She said this to Jesus: "Lord, help me." And Jesus said, "Great is your faith! Be it done for you as you desire." And her daughter was healed.

Did she have an elaborate or impressive plea? No. She said, "Lord, help me." And the Lord heard her and helped her.

Over the course of these 10 chapters, there will be 10 prayers. They all begin with: "Lord, help me..." Because the success of your ministry hinges upon God's blessing and the Holy Spirit's power upon what you do.

Too often we try to do God's work in our own power. We try to carry the weight ourselves only to find that we fall short; only to find that we are left empty handed, or that we don't accomplish what we want or desire. God never intended for you to do ministry alone. He wants to help you. He has given you the Holy Spirit to empower you to do what he has called you to do. It requires you and I to lean in on Him. Just as the Canaanite woman knew nothing to say but, "Lord, help me," I want to remind you today that there are 10 important areas in which we desperately need the Lord's help. And when the Lord empowers us in these 10 areas, our lives and ministries are forever changed.

The change you've been looking for in your ministry can be found in 10 simple sentences. When you pray through them every day and if you will commit to grow in your skills in these areas, these sentences can forever change the way you live, the way you view people, and the way you do ministry. And you know what? Some of the results may not be seen until eternity. I can't wait to dig into Sentence No. 1.

NO. 1

"Lord, help me love people the way you love them."

FIRST JOHN 3:14 SAYS, "We know that we have passed out of death into life, because we love the brothers."

Sentence No. 1 that can revolutionize your ministry is: Lord, help me love people the way You love them.

Your success in ministry hinges on your ability to love and relate well with other people. It's been said that the best thing about ministry is the people and the worst thing about ministry is the people. Right? Ministry is all about people so we need to pray that God will give us a greater capacity to love people.

Leviticus 19:18 says, "You shall not take vengeance or bear a grudge against the sons of your own people, but you shall love your neighbor as yourself: I am the Lord."

In Titus 3:2, Paul commanded Titus to "speak evil of no one, to avoid quarreling, to be gentle, and to show perfect courtesy toward all people." I've learned that 80% of people who fail in ministry fail because they don't know how to love people.

Zig Ziglar, the great entrepreneur, talked about the reasons people get promoted in their work. He said that 15% of people are promoted because of their skills at work. You would think that the opposite would be true. It's natural to think that the reason most people are promoted is because they've learned the skills. And so, because they've learned the skills, they get promoted. But Zig Ziglar says, no, that only accounts for 15%. He said that 85% of people who get promoted at work get promoted because of their relational skills, not their technical skills. So much of your success in life hinges upon your ability to love people.

Jesus modeled this for us. He spent three years of his life on earth teaching us how to love and relate to people. In the introduction, I referred to Matthew 15:25, where the Canaanite woman went to Jesus regarding her daughter who had been demon possessed and was in trouble. She knew nothing to say except for these three words, "Lord, help me." And because of her great faith, Jesus answered her prayers. One of the greatest prayers you can pray as a children's ministry leader is, Lord, help me love people the way you love them.

Here are eight ways to love people the way Jesus loves people.

NO. 1: DON'T COMPLAIN

Philippians 2:14 says to do everything without grumbling and arguing. You've probably experienced this situation. You're talking with people and when you ask how they're doing, they reply, "Oh, I can't complain." And then what do they start doing? They start complaining. "I'm doing well, but my boss..." Or, "Things are fine, but you wouldn't believe what my husband/wife did." We live in a world full of negativity, full of complaints. And what a breath of fresh air it is to be around someone who doesn't complain.

I discovered a website recently named acomplaintfreeworld. org. If you go there, you're challenged to go 21 days without complaining which is difficult for many people. People tend to react negatively to negative people and toxic talk. So instead of being negative and instead of complaining, offer potential solutions when you identify problems. Or, as difficult as it can be, don't say anything at all.

Save it for your journal. That's where you can vent your frustrations. Don't go around venting to everybody. If you will choose not to be a complainer, it can revolutionize your ministry.

NO. 2: SIMPLY SMILE

Ephesians 6:7 says we are to be "rendering service with a good will as to the Lord and not to man."

You've probably heard it said that it takes more muscles to frown than it does to smile. If you search the Internet, the statistics are all over the map. Some people say it takes 50 muscles to frown and it only takes about 13 to 15 muscles to smile. Nobody seems to agree on the numbers, but I do know this: no one wants to be around someone who's constantly frowning, but people enjoy being around people who smile.

I have a question for you: what does your expression tell the world? Does your expression tell the world that you're friendly and approachable, or does your expression tell the world that you're busy and don't have time or interest in people? Practice smiling and you'll be amazed at how people respond to you.

NO. 3: BE A GOOD LISTENER

Proverbs 1:5 says, "A wise man will listen and increase his learning, and a discerning man will obtain guidance."

This is often hard for pastors and ministry leaders. Why? Because we're the leaders, and we're the ones tasked with fixing things. It's our job to solve problems. It's our job to jump in with solutions. It's our job to connect the dots. And it's often very challenging to sit back and listen. Let me encourage you to make every effort possible to listen to everything being said to you. Choose to be an active listener.

By the way, you can tell if someone is listening to you by whether he or she chooses to make eye contact with you. If someone is listening to me, but he's looking everywhere else or he's checking his phone, I wonder if he's really paying to me. And when you're faced with a conflict (which happens in ministry, doesn't it?) instead of responding immediately with your plan of action, choose to listen to what is being said to you. Be a good listener.

NO. 4: BE AN ENCOURAGER

As a children's ministry leader, learn to encourage your volunteers, your pastor, and the parents. Today's parents need encouragement. Amen? Your pastor needs encouragement. The people you serve with need encouragement. Be an encourager. 1 Thessalonians 5:11 says this: "Therefore encourage one another and build one another up." Be the biggest cheerleader in your ministry. It's not just your pastor's job. It's not just your boss's job. Don't have that attitude. Choose to be the biggest cheerleader in your ministry. Choose to champion the kids. Choose to champion the volunteers. Choose to do something every day to help the people around you. Every day you and I can make someone's day better or worse, and often it's dictated solely by the words we say.

NO. 5: BE THANKFUL

If you want to love people, learn to appreciate them and be thankful. First Thessalonians 5:18 says, "Give thanks in everything for this is God's will for you in Jesus Christ." Be thankful. When you benefit from other people's work, teaching, or efforts, let them know you appreciate them. It's been said that if you want more volunteers, make heroes of the ones you already have.

Learn to be thankful and to express that thankfulness. Unexpressed appreciation is un-appreciation. You may know that you appreciate someone. You may know in your heart that you're thankful. But are you expressing it? Send thank-you cards. Send text messages. Send e-mails. Make phone calls. Give $5 gift cards to coffee or ice cream shops. Look people in the eye and tell them how much you appreciate them. If there is anywhere that you should be generous as a leader, it should be with your praise. Be generous by pouring on praise and constantly being wind behind someone's sails.

NO. 6: BE INTERESTED

If you're going to love people the way Jesus loves them, it's going to require you to be interested in those around you. Be genuinely interested in others. Proverbs 27:2 says, "Let another praise you, and not your own mouth." Too many times we feel like we have to praise ourselves and let people know what we've done so we get credit. So, in our conversations, we look for ways to share what we've done instead of being interested in what the other person is saying.

But we need to remember this: my dad always told me that if you're really good at something, you're not going to have to tell anyone about it. People will know. Jesus came, the Bible says, not to be served but to serve and to give himself a ransom for many. So, rather than hoping for opportunities to tell people what you've accomplished, set yourself to the side and be interested in those around you.

Here's the thing: when you're really interested in those around you and when you're really interested in what's happening in their lives and what they're passionate about, the opposite will happen. They will become interested in you, and they will become interested in what you care about and what you are passionate about.

NO. 7: LEARN PEOPLE'S NAMES

If you're going to love people the way Jesus loves them, you're going to have to learn people's names. Song of Solomon 1:3 says, "Your name is oil poured out." Dale Carnegie said this: "Remember that a person's name is, to that person, the sweetest and most important sound in any language." People love to hear their name. Do whatever it takes to learn people's names.

As a children's ministry leader, it's gotten easier to learn kids' names because many churches have systems to print name tags when the kids are checked in. If your church doesn't have the computer program to print out name tags each week, get clip-on tags.

For me, the easiest way to memorize someone's name is by using repetition. I approach memorizing someone's name the same way I approach scripture memory. If I want to memorize a Bible verse, I repeat it over and over and over again. If I want to memorize someone's name, I repeat it over and over and over again.

Here's another method I use: Let's say I meet you at church and I say, "Corey, it was great to meet you today," and I walk away. Three seconds later I've already forgotten Corey's name. But if when I'm meeting Corey, I say, "Corey, I'm so glad to meet you. Is this your first time at our church, Corey? Corey, do you have any brothers or sisters who came with you? Oh, you've got a sister, Corey? Corey, what grade are you in? Corey, you know what? I'm so glad you're here. Corey, come up and see me at the end. I'm going to give you a prize, Corey." Now I have said Corey's name at least eight times. And now what happens when I walk away? I remember Corey's name. Learn people's names.

FINALLY, NO. 8: BE KIND

First Corinthians 13:4 says that love is kind. Kindness is critical to any ministry or any organization. Leaders who are kind to their employees bring employees who are kind to their customers, and their customers become loyal and enthusiastic. Leaders who are kind to their volunteers find that their volunteers are kind to the people they serve. They also tend to stick around. And the people they serve tend to stick around.

What does that mean practically? Don't interrupt people when they talk. Open the door for people. Look people in the eye. Don't tell people they're wrong. Don't gossip. Learn to bite your tongue. Learn to pat people on the back and tell them to have a great day. Look people in the eye and tell them you appreciate them and you're praying for them.

You know, I'm going to throw in two bonus points here, two extra things you can do to love people the way Jesus loves them.

BONUS ITEM NO. 1: LEARN HOW TO RESOLVE CONFLICTS QUICKLY

Conflicts are going to arise in ministry. Why? Because there are people in ministry. Wherever there are people, there are going to be conflicts. Wherever there's motion, there's going to be friction. It's essential to know how to be an effective mediator. Assume the position of a peacemaker, of a mediator, and you will gain respect.

It's so easy as pastors and ministry leaders to sweep things under the rug my head and hope the problems fix themselves. The problem is that they don't usually fix themselves. Learn to solve problems and resolve conflicts when they're little because it's much easier to control a spark than a blazing fire. The apostle Paul said that one of the ministries we have through the Holy Spirit is the ministry of reconciliation. Choose to be a peacemaker. Choose to resolve conflicts as soon as possible. When you resolve conflicts, you show people that you really love them and that you're genuinely committed to them.

BONUS ITEM NO. 2: EXAMINE YOURSELF FREQUENTLY

Ask yourself where you can improve. What's not working in your life? What is working in your life? Take inventory and look at where can you grow and change to love people more.

Ask your spouse. Ask your assistant. Ask the people you work with because here's the thing: we often become blind to our own weaknesses. You know what a blind spot is? Something that you can't see and you don't even really know that you can't see it. So you have to ask other people to speak into your life and tell you about your blind spots.

FINAL THOUGHT

Pastor Rick Warren from Saddleback Church said this: "One of the most important issues every pastor must decide is whether you want to impress people or influence them. You can impress people from a distance, but you have to get up close to people and love people to influence them." If you really want to influence people, you must get close to them and you must love them.

The kids in your ministry don't need a programmer. They don't need someone who can schedule great activities for them. They need a pastor to love them; a shepherd to care for them. So, grow in your love for people. Pray that every day God would give you a greater capacity to love people. If you want to be a success in ministry, you need to pray every day, Lord, help me love people the way you love them.

MY TAKEAWAYS

MY TAKEAWAYS

MY TAKEAWAYS

MY TAKEAWAYS

SENTENCE

NO. 2

"Lord, help me keep my family first."

I N THE LAST CHAPTER, our focus was on asking the Lord to help us love people the way He loves them. I hope it was an encouragement to you and that you will work on being kind and loving to everyone around you, treating them like Jesus would treat them.

Now we're ready for Sentence No. 2. This sentence could change everything for you and your ministry: Lord, help me keep my family first. I've heard it a thousand times: don't sacrifice your family on the altar of ministry. We've all seen Christian and church leaders do this very thing. They run non-stop. They go, go, go. They serve people. They build ministries and programs only to look back one day and realize that they sacrificed their family in the process.

No one wants that. People don't go into ministry hoping they'll lose their kids because of their ministry. People don't go into ministry hoping they'll lose their marriage because they give all they have to church and leave little for their spouses.

The Bible gives some very stern warnings and reminders about keeping family first. First Timothy 5:8 says, "But if any-one does not provide for his relatives, and especially for mem-bers of his household, he has denied the faith and is worse than an unbeliever." Those are strong words, and they should cause us to pause and reflect on how are we doing at home.

Proverbs 11:29 says, "Whoever troubles his own household will inherit the wind." Think about that. What kind of inheritance is the wind? You can't even touch it. There is no real value to it. People who bring ruin on their family will only inherit wind.

None of us wants to ruin our family. None of us wants to become infidels in God's eyes because we have not taken care of our families.

Here's the simple reality: twenty-five years from now, people might remember your church name, but they're not going to remember everything you did. Twenty-five years from now they're not going to remember that Vacation Bible School you ran or that family camp you organized. They're not going to remember all the extra hours you put in. But let me tell you something very important: twenty-five years from now your kids will remember whether you were present in your home and in their lives. And not just present physically but also present emotionally and spiritually. Your spouse will remember whether you were supportive. A pastor friend once told me that you can always get another ministry, but you cannot always get another family.

I want to be very firm while being very loving when I say this: you can lose your family while serving the Lord in ministry. You must choose to keep your family first. The challenge between ministry and family is nothing new. In fact, it goes back to Adam and Eve.

We know God created family. We know God created ministry. God's desire for you is that you steward both. But if you are going to steward both, and steward both well, you have to be intentional. You have to work hard at making sure your ministry does not trump your family.

Now, which should be a priority: ministry or family? Although you would agree, probably whole-heartedly, that family should be the first priority, the simple reality is that we can let our work and ministry dominate our time. And we know what can happen when we choose to make work a higher priority than our family. The results can be devastating.

I think of David in the Old Testament. King David, known as being the man after God's own heart and as being the anointed one, messed up his family. Second Samuel says that in the first twenty years of his reign, David was on fire. He was killing it as a king and leader. However, during those important days when his kids were at home, he neglected them. His family was a mess. David's son, Amnon raped his sister. His other son Absalom, in anger, killed Amnon for what he did. That same Absalom led a rebellion against David.

Here's my point: when you study the life of David, you find that, yes, he was a man after God's own heart. Yes, he was anointed. But, he was also a man who was overly-occupied with his work when his kids were at very impressionable ages. So, here's a question: how are you doing? Are you keeping your family first? Maybe you are, but it's a struggle.

Let me give you five tips to help you keep your family first.

NO. 1: CHOOSE TO BE ACCOUNTABLE TO YOUR SPOUSE

Place yourself under the accountability of your spouse. Gary Smalley talks about this along with John Trent in their book *Love Is a Decision*. Gary Smalley says,

I actually began to prioritize my life from zero to ten, zero being something of little value, ten something of highest value. I established God and my relationship with Christ as the highest, a ten. On a consistent basis, I began looking at my spiritual life and asking the question, "One to ten, where is my spiritual life with Christ?" "How highly do I value His word?" "Prayer?" "Sharing my faith?" Then I placed

*Norma, my wife, above everything else on this earth, way up
in the nines. With this relationship, too, I often asked myself
(and Norma), how am I doing at making you feel like you're
up in the high nines above every one of my hobbies and
friends, and favorite sports teams? What can I do to keep
you believing you're a high nine?*

For many people, conceptualizing issues in numeric terms
is useful. Whatever you want to list (spouse, kids, household
chores, hobbies, etc.), put a numeric value to each item/per-
son, one being the most important and ten being the least, and
assign a number to each.

I have to believe that you would attach the highest value to
your spouse and kids. But what does that look like practically?
Because you can say your wife and kids are number one but if
you're spending more time and energy on ministry, hobbies,
and sports and your kids are getting the scraps, in reality, they
aren't number one. You get my point.

I encourage you to have some open and honest conversations with your spouse. Speak the truth in love and listen with
grace. Ask your kids if they feel like they're getting your best.

NO. 2: REMEMBER THAT PRESENCE ALWAYS TRUMPS PRESENTS

Many people work incredible hours. They have a ministry job
and they have second job. They're hustling and working so
they can give their families the best of everything. We want
to have a great house. We want to eat good food. We want our
kids to have toys. We want them to have the greatest phones,
tablets, and computers. We want them to have a great education, and we want to have a nice car. We work for all this stuff,
meanwhile, we neglect to offer the best of ourselves to our
spouses and children. Our work gets the best us and we give
our families the leftovers.

Listen, at the end of the day, there is something much more
important than the gifts you give your kids. You need to give

them you. A friend once told me that when you're at home, when you're with your kids and spouse, you need to be there. When you're there, be wholly there. Be present.

Now, it's one thing if you have to work extra out of necessity. If it's a matter of needing to pay the mortgage and feed the family, that's a different story and hopefully the extra work is temporary. But if you're working primarily for indulgence's sake, that's another thing. I heard Billy Graham talk one time about how many people overwork and say they're doing it for their family because they love them. He said that not spending time with your wife and children is one of the most unlovable things you can do.

I hope I'm presenting this to you as a velvet hammer. I know this hurts. I know this convicts. I'm convicted as I write. But we all need to hear it. I hope you're receiving it in the love and grace and humility with which I am attempting to deliver it.

NO. 3: WHEN YOU THINK ABOUT YOUR FAMILY, FOCUS ON BOTH QUALITY AND QUANTITY TIME

I've heard parents say, "Well, what really matters is quality time, not necessarily the quantity of time." I think kids need both.

James Dobson said this:

> *Let's suppose you are very hungry having eaten nothing all day. You select the best restaurant in the city and ask the waiter for the finest steak on his menu. He replies that the filet mignon is the house favorite, and you order it charcoal broiled medium rare. The waiter returns 20 minutes later with the fare and sets it before you. There in the center of a large plate is a lonely piece of meat one-inch square flanked by a single piece of potato. You complain vigorously to the waiter, Is this what you call a steak dinner?*

Then he replies, Sir, how can you criticize us before you taste that meat? I brought you one-square-inch of the finest steak money can buy. It is cooked to perfection, salted with care, and served while hot. In fact, I doubt you could get a better piece of meat anywhere in the city. I'll admit that the serving is small, but after all, sir, everyone knows it isn't the quantity that matters. It's the quality that counts in steak dinners.

Nonsense, you reply.

Both quantity and quality are important. Your spouse needs both. Your kids need both.

Here's how you do it: schedule time with your spouse and kids. Do whatever it takes. Schedule time every day to spend time with those who matter most. Schedule dates with your spouse. Schedule from 6:30-7:00pm each night to talk with your daughter about her day. Schedule 6:00-6:30am each day to have breakfast with your son. It might sound too formal to schedule time with your family, but it's better to schedule it so it happens then to go to bed at the end of the day and realize you missed opportunities to connect with your spouse and kids.

NO. 4: LEARN TO SAY NO

Making more time for your family means compromising time somewhere else in life. Putting your family first means making sacrifices as necessary. Proverbs 15:27 says, "Whoever is greedy for unjust gain troubles his own household." You and I must choose to make sacrifices for our family in an attempt to keep them first. Learn to say no to some things.

For some of us, it's very difficult to say no to ministry work. Your pastor asks you to do something, you say yes. Your friend asks you to do something, you say yes. Someone else in the church asks you to do something, you say yes. You're asked to join this committee, you say yes. Then you find yourself overwhelmed, on the road to burnout, and realizing that your family is suffering.

I learned this secret some years ago: saying no doesn't have to mean never. It can mean no, not right now. So, if I say no to a mission trip, it doesn't mean I'll never go on a mission trip. It can mean that I'm not going with the team that's heading out this summer. Saying no, at this phase in my life, also means I'm not going to golf as often as I want. It doesn't mean I'm never going to golf. It means that I'm saying no for right now. But hopefully there will come a time when I can golf more than I am able right now. Saying no to joining that committee or volunteering on that board doesn't mean I'm never going to join that committee or board. It means that I'm not doing it right now.

The two most powerful words in the English language are "yes" and "no." They're powerful because they determine your destiny and dictate your priorities. If you'll learn to say yes to the right things and no to the wrong things, you are on your way to putting your family first.

NO. 5: ASK GOD FOR HELP

God wants you to do your ministry with excellence. He also wants you serve and love your family with excellence. God wants you to manage your ministry while managing your family. God wants you to succeed. He has written a future for you much better than anything you could ever imagine, so pray and ask Him to help you. So, get on your knees before the Lord and ask Him to guide your thoughts, your words, and your actions.

As a pastor, I've been by many people at their deathbed and I've never heard them say at the end of their life that they regret spending too much time with their family. No one ever says that. I'm thankful for the ministry that God has given me. I have the opportunity of serving great ministry leaders like you through our magazine, my books, my speaking, Kidmin Academy, and all the great platforms the Lord has given me to help leaders. But let me tell you something. I want to be famous at home first and foremost. My girls will never read my resume. My wife doesn't care how many people follow me on Twitter or Facebook. I want to succeed at home first and foremost.

FINAL THOUGHT

Let me challenge you: don't allow the enemy to keep you so busy that you lose the most important people in your life. I heard a pastor say that Jesus died for the church so you don't have to. You don't have to die for the church. You don't have to sacrifice your family for the church.

As I said earlier, when you're at home, be at home. Ask God every day to help you put your family first. As you do that, I believe God will answer your prayer. As you ask God for wisdom in grace and strength, and you work to prioritize your family, God is going to answer you and empower you.

Finally, let me recommend one book. It's Andy Stanley's book, *Choosing to Cheat.* The subtitle is *Who Wins When Family and Work Collide?* Andy Stanley says that there will always be something not getting as much of your attention as you think it needs or deserves. He encourages pastors and leaders not to cheat their families.

Remember, you can always get another ministry, but you can't always get another family. Don't neglect your family. You must more intentional than ever before because there are more distractions than ever before.

MY TAKEAWAYS

MY TAKEAWAYS

_____

_____

_____

_____

_____

_____

_____

_____

_____

_____

_____

_____

_____

_____

_____

_____

_____

_____

_____

_____

_____

MY TAKEAWAYS

MY TAKEAWAYS

"Lord, help me to be productive every day"

DO YOU EVER GET to the end of the day and feel like you weren't productive? Like you didn't accomplish the things you wanted and needed to accomplish?

The sentence that can revolutionize your ministry for this chapter is: Lord, help me be productive every day. Just like anyone else, I battle distraction and what I call "opportunity overwhelm" on a daily basis. I'm an idea guy. I get a lot of ideas but then I get distracted. I work on several things at once, and people call me or email me more ideas and I end up with a lot of projects happening at once. I have a lot of plates spinning in the air. And then I see some shiny object and boom, I turn my head toward that shiny object and run after it. And then boom, I see another shiny object and go after that. If I'm not careful, I can find myself running on a treadmill that's going nowhere.

God's desire for you and me as ministry leaders is that we stay productive. Productivity is one thing we should work toward and strive for. My life verse is Colossians 3:23. It says, "Whatever you do, work heartily, as for the Lord and not for men." We need to work with all our hearts and be productive.

Now, sometimes we get confused and we think that we're being productive if we're busy. But busyness doesn't mean that you're producing. Remember the story in Luke 10 of Mary and Martha? When Jesus arrived what was Martha doing? She was running and busy while Mary sat the feet of Jesus. When Martha expressed frustration, Jesus affirmed Mary and addressed Martha. Being busy does not equal productivity.

As ministry leaders, you and I must hone our skills in this area of being focused. The more focused I am, the more productive I will be. And the battle to stay focused as a ministry leader is a battle that wages daily. Unfortunately, it's a fight that never ends this side of eternity. So, how can you be productive? I have 10 tips. I believe, as you do, that as you ask the Lord to lead your steps, you will find that you are getting a lot more done in, perhaps, a lot less time and with less stress.

NO. 1: GET A GOOD NIGHT'S SLEEP

And not just occasionally. As often as humanly possible. It's no secret that a good night's sleep is a key to a great and productive day. Doctors tell us that the average adult needs to get eight to nine hours of sleep a night. I've always been amazed by people who can get by on just four or five hours of sleep a night and maybe a 30-minute power nap. That's never worked for me. I'm the kind of person who needs eight hours each night, and more than likely you are that way too.

Did you know that when you sleep, your brain literally recharges? It's kind of like plugging your phone in at night so that in the morning it's fully charged. Your brain needs to recharge, and to recharge, it needs sleep. I know you probably have kids and they get up early. I have kids who need to get up for school. Many of us can't sleep in like we used to, or we have to get up at 5:00 a.m. for work. Here's a secret I learned from Wayne Cordeiro in his book *Leading on Empty*. Wayne encourages you to sleep in on the front side of the clock. In other words, maybe you're used to getting eight hours of sleep, and, boy, it would sure be nice to get an extra hour or two now and then. But you know you can't sleep in till 8:00

a.m. You have to get up at 6:00. Well, what about instead of going to bed at 10:00, you go to bed at 9:00? What you've done is you've gotten an extra hour of sleep, but you've slept in on the front side of the clock.

The mindset of starting your next day the evening before is something you'll hear me talk about through this book. And I believe it's something you'll find in the Bible. Your day shouldn't start in the morning. Your day should actually start in the evening. We'll talk more about that when we get to point No. 3.

If we go to Genesis 1, we see that God started each day in the evening, not the morning. He said the evening and the morning were the next day. Your day doesn't have to start when you get up. Your day can start the evening before.

NO. 2: STAY OFF ELECTRONIC DEVICES FIRST THING IN THE MORNING

It's so easy to roll out of bed or roll over in bed, grab your phone, and start checking email, Facebook, and Twitter and then start reading your blogs. Then you get to the office, and the very first thing you do is check email. Let me encourage you to resist the temptation to get sucked into checking your email or social networks first thing in the morning.

Here's what happens, especially when you check your email first thing in the morning: you allow other people to set your agenda for the day. Now, if you have a customer service job and your job is to check email first thing in the morning, you better check email first thing in the morning. Otherwise, wait an hour or two to check email or social networks. I'll dig into this more when we get into No. 3, but here's the deal: if I check my email first thing in the morning, I immediately begin to respond, and I allow for other people to set my agenda for my day.

Carl Sandburg said this: "Time is the coin of your life. It is the only coin you have, and only you can determine how it will be spent. Be careful lest you let other people spend it for you." Only you can manage your time. Only you can control your schedule. Wait until at least mid-morning before you start checking email or other social networks. Ephesians 5:15-16 says this: "Look carefully then how you walk, not as unwise but as wise, making the best use of the time, because the days are evil."

NO. 3: PLAN YOUR DAY, PLAN YOUR WEEK

Dale Carnegie said that an hour of planning can save you ten hours of doing. Begin your week by planning your week. I always do this on Sunday nights. I shouldn't say "always." Eight weeks out of ten I plan my week on Sunday evenings. I take one hour to think about the big things I need to accomplish and set high-level priorities for the week. I always keep it around ten things. No more than ten. If I start making a list of more than ten things, I set myself up for defeat. I want to scratch off as many of those things as I can through the week.

So, begin your week by planning your week, and then begin every day by planning your day. Some of you have heard me teach this before, but the first thing I do every day when I get to my office is I fill out a sheet. I call it my productivity planner. In fact, I'll share this with you if you go to ryanfrank.com/productivity. There, you can download my productivity sheet. I use it to write down the people I need to contact and what the priorities are for the day – the things I need to get done no matter what. And then once I've contacted those people, once I've worked on those priorities, then I list some things I can do to move some projects forward.

Now, I understand that in ministry you can plan your day and your week, but all it takes is one phone call or knock on the door and all the planning goes out the window. But if you don't have a target in mind for where you want to go with the day, I know this: you'll never hit anything. You must choose how you want to spend your day. That productivity sheet has been a lifesaver for me. It helps me prioritize what I need to do every day.

NO. 4: AVOID MEETINGS WHEN POSSIBLE

If you're leading a meeting, make sure you have a clear agenda. Make sure you end the meeting with clear and doable action points. I spend a lot of my life in phone meetings and face-to-face meetings, and I want them to be effective and short. So, I want to know who is driving the meeting the goals that need to be accomplished. And at the end of the meeting, we need to know the action points and who is responsible for each action point. Knowing the driver, the goals and the action points helps ensure you actually get things done. Jim Wideman says that often in meetings, more gets said than what gets done. I see you nodding your head in agreement.

NO. 5: DON'T PROCRASTINATE

In my office, I have a piece of paper with this acronym: P.I.T.T.O.T., and it stands for procrastination is the thief of time. Here's what that means: a lot of times we procrastinate because we think we're so busy in the moment that we'll do whatever it is we're putting off at a later time. But in reality, procrastinating costs me more time over the long haul because I put things off. And then because I have put them off, when I finally do get to them, I'm either sloppy when I delegate or they cost me more time because I'm farther away than when I should have actually done them. I forget details which costs me more time. It also robs me of time. So, don't procrastinate. Instead, just be committed to getting things done.

David Allen, a productivity guru who you can find online, teaches something that he calls his two-minute rule. I love his two-minute rule. It pretty much says this: if you think of something to do and you can get it done in two minutes or less, don't bother writing it on your to-do list. Just do it. If you need to talk to somebody quickly or run out to the car to get something or you need to send a quick email, you end up taking two minutes writing it on your to-do list; right? Just get it done. Proverbs 27:1 says, "Do not boast about tomorrow." You don't know what a day may bring. You don't know what's going to happen tomorrow, so don't procrastinate. Just get things done. Some of the most productive people are those who have learned not to procrastinate. Instead, move items forward and get things done.

NO. 6: DISCONNECT FROM THE INTERNET

We are so connected to the internet these days. Our computers, our mobile devices. Some of us drive cars that connect to the Internet or have connection capabilities. We have to be connected at all times. We spend time on social networks, and we waste time on email. The Internet can keep you occupied and unproductive for hours on end. So, have times when you disconnect from the Internet and get things done. Have scheduled times when you're going to check your email, and only let yourself check your blog or surf the web when you have a certain number of things done. For some of you, it may help if you set a timer. When that timer goes off, you unplug until the next scheduled time.

NO. 7: BE A STARTER

You can't finish well unless you start well, so be a starter. Sometimes God gives you an idea. He gives you a ministry. I want to be a friend with this person. I want to build a relationship with this person. I want to make this shift. I want to make that change. I want to write this. I want to do that. But we never start. The hardest part is often just starting, right? I have found that if I can just get moving on a project, even if it's just for a couple minutes, all the sudden that project gets easier and less daunting. I know it's difficult when a project or an idea seems difficult or complex. But if you can take even a couple steps in the right direction, get a little bit of momentum moving, you're going to find it easier to take the next step and the next step and the next step. Be a starter.

Some of you have some great ideas that God has put on your heart. A great vision or great plans that you would like to do one day. Just get started. Don't take those ideas, visions, projects, programs, or ministries to your grave without doing them. Choose to be a starter.

NO. 8: LEARN TO SAY NO

I talked about this some in the last chapter, but let me remind you once again that the two most powerful words in the English language are "yes" and "no" because they determine your destiny and they dictate your priorities. Learn to say no.

I know some of you have a really hard time with this. It's not very complicated – but I know that it can feel complicated. But hear me out - when I learn to say no to some things, it gives me the margin to say yes to other things. When you constantly say yes to everything that comes your way, you'll find yourself in trouble. You're more likely to experience stress, burnout, and possibly even depression. So, learn to say no to allow yourself to have the margin and freedom to say yes to things you really want to accomplish.

NO. 9: EAT THE FROG FIRST

Yep, you read that right. Mark Twain said this, "Eat a live frog first thing in the morning and nothing worse will happen to you the rest of the day." It's really nice to do the fun, easy things first. It's much less fun to do the difficult tasks first in the day. But here's the secret: if you can do the difficult tasks first, everything else will be easy. So make yourself do the difficult things first. And once you have those things done, allow yourself to do the fun stuff.

When you set your priorities for the day, choose to do the most difficult things first. That will keep you away from the trap of procrastinating, and it will set you on the road to pro-ductivity in getting done what you need to get done.

NO. 10: USE GOOD TOOLS

You are as effective as the tools in your toolbox, so learn to find, implement, and use good tools daily. I love my iPhone. I love my MacBook Pro because they are tools that help me do my ministry well. I organize my to-do list in Todoist. Todoist.com is an app and website. It synchronizes my to-do lists between all my devices. I keep my notes in Evernote. I use it to take all my meeting notes and input all my ideas – everything gets dumped into Evernote. I especially love the search functionality of Evernote. I can take a picture of a business card or a handwritten note, put it in Evernote, and Evernote can search my handwriting.

I want to encourage you to use good tools. Maybe your tool is a simple legal pad. Maybe it's a Post-It® note system. There's no right tool or wrong tool. Just find tools that work for you. The important thing is that you evaluate your tools to make sure you are being effective.

FINAL THOUGHT

Here's the main takeaway as I wrap up this chapter: we're all busy. It's a matter of setting the right priorities and asking the Lord to help you be productive every day. And that is key: asking the Lord to help you be productive every day. Proverbs 16:9 says, "The heart of man plans his way, but the Lord establishes his steps." Plan your day and ask the Lord to direct you along the way. You must to live by your priorities. You must choose every day that by God's grace and strength, you're going to be productive so you can grow your life and ministry, and do it faster and more effectively than ever before.

MY TAKEAWAYS

MY TAKEAWAYS

MY TAKEAWAYS

MY TAKEAWAYS

_____

_____

_____

_____

_____

_____

_____

_____

_____

_____

_____

_____

_____

_____

_____

_____

_____

_____

_____

_____

_____

_____

_____

SENTENCE

NO. 4

"Lord, help me
to step back and
evaluate what
matters most."

HERE WE ARE IN CHAPTER 4. I trust you've enjoyed the training so far. Thank you for allowing me to help you in your ministry to kids and families.

Today we're going to learn about a sentence that can revolutionize everything for you, and that is, Lord, help me to step back and evaluate what matters most.

I read a story about Kemmons Wilson. Kemmons was the founder of Holiday Inn. Someone once asked him about the secret to his success. Kemmons said, "That's a really good question. You know, I never really had a college education. I've always only worked half a day. So I guess my advice would be this: only work half days. Now, you choose. Is it going to be the first 12 hours of the day or the second 12 hours of the day?"

Here's why I share that story: some of the most hard-working people are children's ministry leaders and pastors. We work so hard, and we have to be on all the time. But here's the question: Are we stepping back to evaluate how we spend our time and energy to make sure we're effective?

One of my favorite people in the Bible is Nehemiah. He has such an inspiring story. We know the background of

Nehemiah: King Nebuchadnezzar had destroyed Jerusalem 152 years prior. He had knocked down the walls of the city and burned the city gates. After some time, the Israelites were allowed to go back home after having been displaced. But they didn't start rebuilding the walls when they got back home from Babylon and that left them very vulnerable and open to enemy attack.

Then Nehemiah entered the story. Nehemiah was a cup-bearer to the king of Persia and was well respected. He had a vision and the burden to go back home and restore the city to its former grandeur. So, he asked for and received the king's blessing and went home to help rebuild the walls. Unfortunately, this job came with considerable opposition. Not only toward Nehemiah but toward the other workers. In fact, they had to work with a sword in one hand and a hammer in the other. They had to be prepared to fight while they worked.

Despite the opposition, Nehemiah rebuilt the walls of Jerusalem. It was an overwhelming undertaking that required skilled management. Nehemiah managed the different families and people, and they ended up getting the job done in 52 short days.

Why do I tell you this story? Because Nehemiah understood the importance of three P's that we're going to talk about in this chapter: people, programs, and processes. Nehemiah built a team of people. He identified the programs needed. And he put processes in place to make sure that things got done.

NO. 1: EVALUATE YOUR PEOPLE

Think of a triangle. I first saw this idea in training from Sam Chand. When you look at yourself and the people you serve, there are four groups of people within this triangle. You have your thinkers, your organizers, your doers, and finally, the crowd (everyone else).

First let's talk about your thinkers. You can also describe them as dreamers. This is where you and a small group needs to be. Jesus had His thinkers, His dreamers. Jesus had His three. He had Himself and Peter, James, and John. These beloved disciples were with Him during the high points like at the Mount of Transfiguration. They were also with Him during the low points like in the Garden of Gethsemane.

Second, think about your organizers. Jesus had the 12, the organizers. These might be your department leaders, your ministry leaders. The people you rely on to oversee projects and ministries. Now, the only way you can be a thinker or a dreamer and have the margin is to make sure you have organizers. You've found them, you've equipped them and developed them, and then you've deployed them.

Third, think about your doers. You need doers. Everyone needs doers. Otherwise you're going to be living as a doer when you need to be up higher in the triangle as a thinker. Jesus had doers. He had the 70 like those in John 10.

Finally, there's the crowd – everyone else. Jesus had his crowd. For the sake of our conversation, we'll refer to this as the people we serve. The kids, the families, and the congregation.

Here's what you need to do as a children's ministry pastor or leader: you need to be moving people up the pyramid. Many children's pastors and leaders are living as doers or organizers.

You need to recruit people to be organizers and doers. And then you need to find the cream of the crop of your organizers and bring them up with you to be a thinker.

So where are you right now? Are you a doer when you should be a thinker?

Here's another question you need to ponder: Do you have the right people in the right place? One reason I want you to understand this triangle is because I want you to think about your people. You have to make sure you have the right people in the right

49

place. Sam Chand says this: "Proper people placement prevents problems. Proper people placement prevents problems."

Listen, if you have someone who's an organizer and you have him doing the work of a doer, he's not going to find satisfaction and fulfillment in that. He's probably going to get frustrated, and migrate to a ministry that will allow him to be an organizer and a doer.

If you have a doer in the role of an organizer, she's going to be way out of her league. She's not going to be able to get done what you want her to get done. You're going to be frustrated and she's going to be frustrated. You want to make sure that you have the right people in the right place on the pyramid.

Final question: What does this pyramid say about the health of your ministry? If you as the leader are living down in the bottom of the triangle as a doer, that tells me something about the health of your ministry.

By the way, the number one indicator of the health of your children's ministry is found in the doer section. The health of your volunteer force shows the health of your ministry and the brunt of your force should be the doers. Are your volunteers showing up on time or showing up early? If they're not, that says something about the health of your ministry. Are your volunteers energetic and full of life, or are they dragging in? That says something about the health of your ministry. Do the volunteers love the kids? Are they committed to the team? Do they have a team spirit? Are they recruiting other volunteers for your children's ministry? The health of your volunteers speaks highly to the health of your ministry.

You have to constantly step back and evaluate your people. One of the greatest things you can learn to do today is to pray, "God, give me the courage, give me the discipline, give me the margin so I can step back and evaluate my people." Your people are the greatest assets in your ministry. They are the lifeblood. If you don't believe it, try to survive this Sunday by yourself with zero volunteers. You need people, you need to make sure you have them in the right place, and you need to make sure that you are in the right place. So first, I want to encourage you to evaluate your people.

NO. 2: EVALUATE YOUR PROGRAMS

There are some things you need to look at constantly; things that need to be on your dashboard.

The first thing to evaluate is your curriculum. Is your curriculum accomplishing what you need it to accomplish? Your curriculum is your road map. Your curriculum gets you from where you are today to where you want to be, where your kids are today to where you want your kids to be. Don't assume that because your denomination publishes a curriculum that it's going to reach the goals God has given you or your ministry. Don't assume because any curriculum is popular that it's going to accomplish the goals you want to accomplish. You have to evaluate it. And don't evaluate it in a vacuum. Evaluate it with other key stakeholders and leaders.

The second thing to evaluate is your discipleship plan. Do you know where your kids are on a discipleship road map? Do you know which kids have made a profession of faith? Do you know which kids have been baptized? Do you know which kids are bringing their Bibles? Do you know what kids are learning at certain age/grade levels?

Are the kids excited? This needs to be on your dashboard. Are they present? I was consulting with a church recently. They had a lot of kids in the main auditorium who should have been in the children's ministry. As I began to talk with people, I found out there was a disconnect. The kids weren't excited about what was going on in the children's ministry. Make sure you're creating a program that the kids are excited about.

What about relationship building strategies? Do you have strategies in place for kids to build good friendships and relationships with each other and with adult leaders?

What about the church-parent partnership? What's your church-parent partnership strategy? Are parents being equipped and encouraged to be the primary spiritual leaders at home? It's one thing to encourage them to do it and it's another thing to equip them.

Parents are the number one spiritual influencers in their kids' lives. Do you know who the number two spiritual influencers are? It's not the church. It's grandparents. Even grandparents who aren't raising their grandchildren play a huge role in the spiritual lives of their grandchildren. What are you doing about that? I want to see more churches develop grandparent strategies.

Larry Fowler, who was once a part of the leadership at Awana created The Legacy Coalition. They host conferences and have created church resources to help grandparents be the best spiritual leaders and influencers they can.

What about special needs ministry? I'm convinced that if your church got serious about loving and welcoming families that have kids with special needs your church will see growth. There are families in your community that have children with special needs, but they don't know what to do with them on Sundays, and they don't know that your church welcomes them and has a plan for their children and would love to have them be a part.

I understand that this can be overwhelming and daunting. As my friend Craig Johnson says, it's 20% training, and 80% love and acceptance. You don't have to have a staff of volunteers who are 100% trained on how to handle special needs children. You need a staff of volunteers who are 80% full of love and acceptance and 20% trained. More than anything, parents want to know that their kids with special needs are loved and accepted.

When you have a children's ministry with an intentional special needs ministry, families will come. There are some great ministries to help you accomplish this. I encourage you to check out Champions Club, which is a ministry of Lakewood Church. I also encourage you to check out Nathaniel's Hope based out of the Orlando, FL, area. Joni Eareckson Tada has a great special needs ministry. Barb Newman has a great special needs ministry called the CLC Network. There are some great resources to help you in your special needs ministry as your church works to develop this.

NO. 3: EVALUATE YOUR PROCESSES

There are five processes you should consistently evaluate.

First, you need to evaluate your visitor experience. Sam Chand says that the first time a family visits your church, they are anxious about the facilities. The second time, they are anxious about the people. It's not until their third visit that their anxiety is lowered and they are more receptive to you and your ministry. So, evaluate and ask yourself what the visitor experience is like through fresh lenses. You might have to bring other people in and ask for some honest feedback.

There are many things and processes to evaluate when it comes to visitors: pulling into the parking lot, entering the front door of the church, walking up to the welcome center, checking in their children to a class, finding the worship center, picking up their children, and finally walking out of the church. We often stop the evaluation process with the kids being dropped off to class. But church isn't over. Make sure you have a great exit strategy. That when the kids are picked up, everything runs smoothly. And when the visitors are leaving the church, they are greeted again and there's a clear path out of the parking lot.

I'll give you one example of something I think is cool. Life Church in Oklahoma has a red bag strategy. When a family visits the church for the first time, they are given a red bag.

It contains information about the ministries of the church. Everyone at church is trained to keep an eye out for red bags. And whenever people see a red bag, they know to go out of their way to meet and encourage the visiting family.

Second, evaluate your check-in and check-out process. You need to make sure your check-in and check-out process is being enforced. I don't know about you, but most churches don't have a problem with checking kids in. Where they have a problem is parents and volunteers failing to check kids out the way they're supposed to. And while your check-in process is important, your check-out process is vital. You have to make sure your volunteers are checking kids out properly, whatever your system is. You must have tight check-out processes because this is one of the times where you and the kids in your ministry are most vulnerable.

So, how do you enforce check-in and check-out processes? You have to constantly communicate the vital processes to your volunteers – and sometimes you need to be there at check-in and check-out to observe. It's difficult to convey the processes and the importance of the processes in meetings because while having a monthly teacher meeting is a good practice, it's hard to get everyone to show up. Email helps but it's hard to get everyone to read their emails. So, you have to do a little bit of everything. You might even want to consider having a five-minute huddle before or after church where you remind volunteers to check-in and check-out the way that's been taught. Encourage volunteers that this process isn't in place for the sake of having another process. It's there to protect kids, parents, volunteers, and the church.

You have to make sure you have two adults in a room at all times. No less than two adults. And you need to make sure that it's not two men or two teenagers. You may have teenagers who are great volunteers and they shine, and you would put them up against any of your adults. That's great. But visiting parents don't know those teenagers the way you do and they don't know how great they are so there's a good chance they aren't as comfortable leaving their kids with a couple teenagers as they would be with a couple of adults or an adult and a teenager. You also want to make sure that you don't have only two men in the room. Again, these men may have passed background checks. They may be great men and leaders in the church, but moms aren't comfortable dropping their kids off in a room with two men. Most sexual crimes are committed by men, so make sure you have a mix with at least one adult and at least one woman. It's a sad reality but you need to protect everyone involved and be above any kind of reproach.

Third, it's important to evaluate your volunteer onboarding and retention. How are your volunteers onboarded? Are they thrown into a room where you lock the door and throw away the key, or do they get to shadow someone for a month and receive training? Do you follow up and make sure it's been a good experience and if where they're serving is a good fit?

What about retention? I've found that a majority of churches and children's ministries don't have a recruiting problem. They have a retention problem. You have to learn how to love and care for volunteers and to create a community. I talk about that in my *Volunteer Code* book. You have to make sure you create a culture and community where you couldn't drive volunteers off with a stick. If you learn how to retain volunteers, you won't have near the problem recruiting volunteers because you won't have as many empty slots.

Fourth, evaluate your environment. What's your environment like? When is the last time you evaluated the process of your environment? Do you have a clean, organized environment? Is it kid-friendly? Now, I want to caution you. I love going into churches where I see cool environments. Some churches have chosen to spend a lot of money creating a Disney-type environment, and that's perfectly fine. But let me tell you something. That's not what matters most to Mom.

What matters most to Mom is that her kids are safe and loved and cared for.

But, environments still matter. You don't have to spend thousands of dollars on a Disney-type environment. But you can spend $20 on a gallon of paint. You can keep things clean. You can keep the walls fresh. We know that when church shopping, environments are high on the menu for visiting families. So, make sure you have great kid-friendly, clean environments.

Fifth, and last, you have to evaluate the safety and security of your ministry and church.

This has to be a priority for you and your children's ministry. Are you running background checks on your volunteers? That's a nonnegotiable.

Is there a security presence during services? Some churches have uniformed or plain-clothes officers patrolling various parts of the church during services. Some churches use dads to patrol. Asking dads to be a part of your security team is a great way to get them involved in your ministry.

FINAL THOUGHT

To wrap up this chapter, as you look at your people, your programs, and your processes, it forces you to ask three questions:

What do we need to start doing right now...in the next month...in the next six months?

What do we need to keep doing?

What do we need to stop doing?

Evaluating is so important. Evaluation, you could say, is the breakfast of champions. You must constantly evaluate your people, your program, and your processes. When you evaluate, you set yourself up to grow and change and improve.

MY TAKEAWAYS

MY TAKEAWAYS

MY TAKEAWAYS

MY TAKEAWAYS

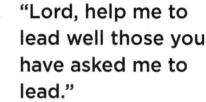

"Lord, help me to lead well those you have asked me to lead."

Gᴏᴅ ɴᴇᴠᴇʀ ɪɴᴛᴇɴᴅᴇᴅ for you to do ministry alone. It's been said that it's lonely at the top. Well, if it's lonely at the top, something is wrong. Bring other people up with you.

This fifth sentence that can revolutionize your ministry is this: Lord, help me to lead well those you've called me to lead.

We often do ministry alone and feel like we're carrying the weight ourselves when what we should be doing is building depth in our team and bringing leaders up. The idea of having a team is a biblical thing. We see it in the New Testament and the Old Testament. Jesus had a team. In Luke 9:1-2, He called the 12 together and gave them power and authority over demons and the power to cure diseases. He sent them out to proclaim the kingdom of God and to heal. Jesus had a team.

Mighty David had his men who could shoot an arrow and sling a stone. Jashobeam, the Hachmonite, was one example. In one famous battle, the "Beam" killed 300 enemy warriors with his spear all by himself.

Daniel's team included his best friends – Hananiah, Mishael, and Azariah. We know them as Shadrach, Meshach, and

Abednego. These great people of the Bible had a team. You need a team.

Too many children's pastors are jacks-of-all-trades. They do a little bit of everything when it comes to managing their ministry. Now, that versatility can be a great asset when you start, but you have to build a team or you will stretch yourself too thin. You will lose heart. You will burn out and never reach your full potential. At some point, if you try to do everything on your own, you will hit a wall.

Moses learned this the hard way. You can read the story in Exodus 18. He was working during the day. He was a judge at night. He was leading, leading, leading. Apparently, it was causing friction at home because his wife went home, and it wasn't much later that Jethro, his father-in-law, gave him some very wise counsel. He told Moses that he needed to build depth.

You need to build depth in your ministry team. God has given you ministry leaders, volunteers, and parents, and it's your job to develop them and build a team to do ministry alongside of you.

LEARN TO DELEGATE

To build depth, you have to learn to delegate. You need to learn to find responsible people who you trust and to give them work. We'll unpack this the idea of delegation in a bit, but first you need to understand why you need to delegate. Delegating accomplishes two things.

First, delegating gets done the things you want done but can't get done. We each have 24 hours in a day. If you feel like you are so busy that you can't get anything more done, you have to start using someone else's time.

Second, delegating gives the person you're delegating to the chance to learn and grow. Delegating can feel scary sometimes – you're responsible for a ministry so if something doesn't get done or goes wrong, it reflects on you. But there was a time when someone took a risk on you. There was a time when someone poured into your life and gave you the opportunity to fail or succeed.

Part of your job as a children's ministry leader is to develop leaders. Delegating is a key to this process. If you're going to begin delegating and leading well those who you are called to lead, you have to start by analyzing your needs. If I were to ask you what the needs of your ministry are right now, I hope you could tell me. You need to know the needs of your ministry for where you are today. You need to know what slots you need filled. You also need to know your needs leading into the future. God has given you a vision. God has given you a dream. And for this dream to become a reality, you need to know what needs to happen.

NO 1: LEARN THE NEEDS OF YOUR MINISTRY

First you need to list the needs. What do you need help with? What do you need to build a strong team? Then move beyond the practicality and into the future.

In the most practical sense, some of you need more help – more bodies to carry more of the load. You're running a children's ministry. You're working a job outside the church. You have kids and you're running them to various places. You volunteer on a board or committee somewhere. Plus, you have some hobbies you'd like to do every so often. You have a lot going on and you need help.

One of the best ways to find out where you need help is to track your time. Take a week and write down what you do every hour of the day. What you'll find when you look back is where your priorities fall and where they don't fall but should. You'll see what you need to stop doing, what you need to start doing, and what you need to keep doing.

I did this recently as I tracked two weeks of my time. I found I'm way too busy checking my email - I was spending five to six hours a day on email. So, I decided that I'm only going to check email three times a day, and I'm getting some help managing email.

When you track your time, you'll also identify areas where others can help. Question: What are you doing that only you can do? Another way of asking that question is, What are you doing that's keeping you from doing what only you can do? There are tasks that other people can do so that you can focus on the things that only you can do.

NO 2: EXPLORE THE OPTIONS

You only have a few options when you think about all the things you have to do.

The first option is to work harder. Instead of working eight-hour days, you work nine. Instead of working nine-hour days, you work ten. You begin to work a ridiculous amount of time to try to get things done. Not the best idea.

The second option is to set priorities. Prioritize what must get done verses what you want to get done but can survive without getting done.

The third option is to talk with your boss. Share the results of the time you tracked and show your boss that there's too much on your plate.

NO. 3: BE SMART ABOUT THE WHO AND WHAT

You have to be smart in the WHO. Remember Moses? He went up on the mountain to talk with God, and what did he do? He left his brother Aaron in charge. Big mistake, right? What happened when Moses returned? Aaron directed the people to put their gold in a pot, melted it, and then molded it into a golden calf. You have to make sure you delegate to the right people. You have to find people you trust, people who are responsible, people who know your heart, and people who represent you and your ministry well. You have to think through who you delegate to or it's going to come back to you. So, you have to be smart in how you delegate. You have to choose the right people.

You also have to be smart in the WHAT. Don't make tasks complicated. Don't delegate the most complicated task on your to-do list. You probably have some big stuff that's a pain, but you know it's stuff that only you can do and it's complicated or complex. You might be able to eventually delegate those tasks, but don't delegate the most complicated tasks right away. Start with things that are fairly easy to learn.

I want you to remember Andy Stanley's four levels of delegation. Each level represents a different degree and type of oversight.

The first level of delegation is investigation. This is how you qualify if people can help you. You task people to investigate something and report back to you. During that investigation process, you find out who is capable. If they come back to the table with lots of ideas and a potential game plan, this is someone you want to have on your team and who you can rely on.

The next level of delegation is informed progress. When you ask people to do something, you tell them to keep you in the loop and keep you updated. Do they follow through and give you updates?

The third level is informed results. Now that you've handed people a task, you trust them to do the investigation. You trust them to make progress and show you the finished result.

The fourth level of delegation, according to Andy Stanley, is ownership. This is where you trust people to be owners of their task. They can fully take the job with little or no oversight. They are truly capable. You know that if you give them a task, they're going to see it through to the end, and you're going to trust them along the way.

Now, remember that you have to take these in the right order. A lot of times we grab warm bodies and give them ownership, but we've skipped levels. Then they drop the ball, and we get upset when the blame really falls on us.

Let me give you another tip as you build a team and lead a team well.

NO. 4: DOCUMENT THE PROCESS

One reason it's easier for you to do things is because you know exactly how they need to be done. You know exactly what the outcome needs to look like, and you know the exact process and systems and steps it takes to get you there. So, as you delegate, you need to document and communicate the steps to people.

How do you communicate? You communicate by sharing a document. Document your check-in and check-out process. Document your curriculum process – how it's ordered, how it's delivered. Document your strategies. Document how you organize VBS and how you clean up. Create documents so that as you build a team, people aren't working blindly. This will help you so much as you train people because there's a cheat sheet. People will be more apt to volunteer and take on more work if they know they will have training and will have documents that tell them exactly what to do.

NO. 5: START TRAINING

If you're going to build a team and lead it well, you have to make sure you spend time onboarding, a word we don't talk a lot about in children's ministry. We talk about recruiting volunteers. We talk about getting volunteers to stick. We talk about how we close the back door so volunteers don't quit. We talk about how to avoid burnout with volunteers. What we don't talk about in children's ministry leadership is how we onboard our volunteers. Onboarding refers to the process of how you get them from the point where they say, "Yes, I will help," to where they are leading and doing what you've asked them to do. There is a process involved.

Now, there isn't one magic process because every ministry is different and the tasks are different. But there needs to be an onboarding road map. Here's what onboarding is not: "Yes, you will volunteer? Okay. There's the room and there's the book." No! You say something like, "I'm going to let you shadow someone. Then we're going to sit down and have coffee and answer your questions. We're going to make sure this is a good fit. After you have been doing this for a month, we're going to meet to make sure you enjoy it and to see if this is where you want to be or do you want to be somewhere else. I'm going to make sure you have the right tools."

Here is the desired end of onboarding: you have a confident and invested leader. You don't have someone who said yes but doesn't have passion for the ministry or the role. You want confident, invested leaders.

NO. 6: CAST THE MINISTRY VISION – CONSISTENTLY AND OFTEN

When you delegate, you explain the why behind the what. When people understand the why, it's easier to remember the what. And as people understand the why, they're more likely to stick around for the long haul.

FINAL THOUGHT

You and I need to build a team. We need to build depth. We need to pray every day, Lord, would you help me to lead well who you've called me to lead. Leading alone is dangerous. 1 Peter 5:8 says that we must be "sober-minded; be watchful. Your adversary the devil prowls around like a roaring lion, seeking someone to devour." When we isolate ourselves and when we're alone, we become more vulnerable to an attack. You must lead well those you have been given to lead. You must build a team and put people in the right places. You need to provide growth opportunities so people can learn and grow together as a team.

If you're going to lead well as a children's ministry leader, you need a team that's beside you and behind you. Leadership is supposed to be plural. If you're called to lead, you are called to lead together. God never intended for you to lead alone. Let me encourage you to be intentional. Work hard every day at leading well those people who God has given you. They're a gift. They're a treasure, and they need to be treated that way.

MY TAKEAWAYS

MY TAKEAWAYS

MY TAKEAWAYS

MY TAKEAWAYS

"Lord, help me see
things and hear things
that others aren't
because they are
looking and listening in
the wrong places."

THE SENTENCE THAT IS the focus of this chapter is: Lord,
help me see things and hear things that others aren't because they're looking and listening in the wrong places.

I know that's a long sentence. Let me say it again. Lord, help
me to see things and hear things that others aren't because
they're looking and listening in the wrong places. I cannot stress
enough how important it is that you look and listen in the right
places to get the answers and help you need for your ministry.

2 Corinthians 4:18 says that we should fix our eyes not on
what is seen, but on what is unseen. In your ministry journey,
you're going to find all kinds of roadblocks that get in the way
of where you want to go and where you want your ministry to
go. Sometimes these roadblocks are people. Sometimes these
roadblocks are systems. Sometimes they're your own fears
and insecurities: those things within you that keep you from
your destiny and where God wants you to go.

A secret to ministry is learning how to push through a road-
block – and the next one, and the next one. How do you push
through these roadblocks? How do you overcome obstacles
in your ministry? One of the greatest ways to push through

roadblocks and to overcome obstacles in your ministry is to learn to ask great questions.

John Maxwell wrote a book by that very title, *Good Leaders Ask Great Questions*. Sometimes knowing the right questions is better than having the right answers. In fact, you could say it this way: the fastest way to change the answers you receive from yourself or others is to change the questions you ask. Questions are a powerful tool. As I learn to ask good questions, I find that obstacles disappear. I find that roadblocks scoot out of the way. And I find that I move farther down the road faster. When you learn to ask the right questions, you will begin to see and hear things other people aren't because you're looking and listening in the right places. I want to share 12 questions you need to ask to overcome roadblocks in ministry and to get where God wants you to go.

THE WRONG AND RIGHT QUESTIONS

No. 1: Why won't these kids listen? Have you ever driven home on Sunday wanting to pull out your hair as you ask yourself, "Why won't these kids just listen!?"

That's the wrong question to ask. The right question to ask is this: Are you as prepared as you could be? I'm convinced that 80% of discipline problems in a classroom with children is the fault of the person in charge. Now, I didn't say 100% but a majority of discipline problems we deal with in children's ministry are the fault of the person in charge. If I'm not prepared for the kids, they will be prepared for me. I have to make sure that I am super prepared, that everything is set up in advance, and that the kids don't know what's coming next.

Now, if you work with early childhood kids, you know that they want structure. They perform better when they know what's coming next. But if you work with elementary age kids, if they can predict what you're doing next, it's a breeding ground for problems. So instead of wondering why the kids won't listen, ask yourself if you're as prepared as you should be. Make sure you have everything set up and ready to go before the kids get there. Make sure that you keep an element of suspense and surprise. Make sure you change things up now and then. Change the schedule so the kids don't know what's coming next. Think through questions the kids are going to ask and how will you answer them.

No. 2: Why do I need to worry about anyone else? My focus is the kids. That's the wrong question to ask. You may be the children's pastor or the children's ministry director, but do those kids bring themselves? No. Their parents bring them. The right question is this: Who do I need to focus on other than the kids?

I've heard Jim Wideman teach this concept before: as a children's ministry leader, you work with four groups of people. Group No. 1: parents. Group No. 2: volunteers. Group No. 3: your pastor or church leadership. Group No. 4: kids. Only one out of four groups that you work with are kids. You can be a great children's pastor and you can be great in front of those kids, but you have to make sure you can relate to adults as well.

Where do you rate when it comes to relating to adults – both parents and volunteers? Are you showing them appreciation? Are you listening to them? Are you talking with them? Are you building relationships? Are you praying for them? Parents need you as an ally. What are you doing to partner with them and encourage them as they parent their kids? What about your pastor and church leadership? How is your communication? Is the church leadership being caught by surprise way too often? Are you staying on budget? Are you aligning what you're doing with the vision of your pastor and church?

See how asking the right question can help you overcome hurdles? Some of you are overcoming big hurdles because you think kids are your main thing. And while you may be called to serve and to minister to kids, you have to learn to grow your relational and interpersonal skills with adults.

No. 3: Why won't my pastor support my vision? You have all these great ideas. All you need is money to buy more stuff! All you want to do is launch a program. Asking why your pastor won't support your visions is the wrong question to ask. The right question to ask is: Am I supporting my pastor's vision?

I've learned that the more I support my pastor's vision, the more my pastor will support my vision. It's very easy as a children's ministry leader to have tunnel vision: you only see what's straight ahead of you and you don't see what's in your peripheral. It's very easy to see your children's ministry, programs, wants, and needs. Your pastor, however, sees everything. He has the big picture. I've learned that if I can connect my dreams and hopes with the heart and vision of my pastor, I have a much better chance of my pastor getting onboard and supporting what I would like to do.

No. 4. Why don't my volunteers have the vision and passion that I have for the ministry? Sometimes you read a book or go to a seminar or a conference and rub shoulders with people in children's ministry, and it gets you all fired up. You're ready to go conquer the world! Then you go back home and are frustrated because your volunteers don't get it. They don't see the vision. The right question to ask is: Have I effectively communicated the vision to my volunteers?

In Habakkuk 2:2, God told the prophet Habakkuk to write down the vision on tablets of stone so people could read them. As the leader, you have to write down your vision simply and communicate it in a way that other people see your vision so they can run with it. God normally gives a vision to a leader. It's your job as the leader to communicate the vision to everyone else. Howard Hendricks said this: "Where there's a mist in the pulpit, there will be a fog in the pews." His point is this: as a leader, you have to speak and communicate with great clarity. Because if there is not great clarity coming from you, there is going to be a lot of questions with those you are leading.

If God has given you a great vision for your children's ministry, it's your job to communicate it and to do so over and over again in multiple ways. Thankfully in this digital age, we have lots of ways to communicate our vision? We have email, texting, and various social networks. Then we have printed pieces, bulletin boards, and the TV monitors around our churches. We have all kinds of ways to communicate the vision and passion.

No. 5: Why won't my church give me more money? First of all, I want to encourage you with something: every church faces budget issues. You might that if you were at a bigger church, you wouldn't have to deal a small budget. But even bigger churches have budget issues. But if you learn to ask the right question and to see and hear things in places other people aren't, you will have a breakthrough.

Instead of asking, why your church won't give you more money, ask: Am I displaying excellence with what God has given me? You see, people are a lot more excited about giving money to a ministry or person that does things with excellence. You have to be committed to excellence. Don't make fund-raising your focus in ministry. If you make fund-raising your focus, it's going to cost you. Do with excellence what God has given you to do. Instead of making fund-raising your focus and complaining that you don't have the money you want, do things with excellence.

It's possible to do things with excellence on a shoestring budget. Did you know that? Because excellence does not have to mean extravagance. I've been in small churches. I've been in old churches. I've been in places that have no money, but they are clean and they do things with excellence, and they make much out of what they have.

One way to do a lot with a little is to double dip: share costs. If you want a specific piece of technology for your children's ministry, see if your youth pastor is interested in going in with you and split the cost. You share it and both ministries benefit.

No. 6: Can I take a break? I'm burning out. The source of this question is your volunteers. If you're in children's ministry and you work with volunteers, you know that people burn out and you've most likely heard this question before.

Here's the right question to ask when someone tells you he or she is burning out: Is there a need in your life that is not being met? When people come to you and say, "I'm burning out," what they're really saying is that there's a need in their life that's not being met. They may not even realize it. Maybe you're feeling burned out right now as you read this chapter. If so, more than likely there's a need in your life that's not being met.

By the way, burnout is not a biblical thing. No one in the Bible ever burned out. People burned up, but no one burned out. Elijah probably came the closest. After the battle against the prophets of Baal on Mount Carmel, and after Jezebel pursued him with the intent to kill him, Elijah hid under a juniper tree and asked God to take his life. So, God sent an angel who told Elijah to get some rest. The angels told him to eat some bread and that he wasn't alone. And that's all Elijah needed. He ate and rested and he picked back up. He was on the verge of burnout because he had needs in his life that weren't being met.

Now, if someone comes to you and says, "I'm feeling burned out. I need a break," you have to give the person a break. It could be something with his or her health. It could be something spiritually. It could be something financial. It could be something at work. It could be problems at home. But there is a need in this person's life that is not being met, and the quicker you can help the person find rest and work through the issue, the quicker you're going to get that volunteer back. If you, as a ministry leader, feel like you're burning out, let me encourage you to evaluate the area/s in your life where needs aren't being met.

No. 7: Why won't more people volunteer? After all, I put clipboards out in the church lobby. I run announcements in the church bulletin. I include something in the newsletter. Why won't more people sign up to volunteer? The right question is this: Why am I not doing more recruiting? Listen, your job is not to try to get people to sign up. Your job is to recruit.

You have to learn the art and the skill of recruiting. How do you recruit? You don't recruit 10 or 15 or 20 people at a time. You recruit like Jesus did. You recruit one or two people at a time. I've talked to people at church of all sizes. I recently talked to the children's pastor at Lakewood Church, the largest church in America, and guess how they recruit? One or two at a time. You have to learn to grow your recruiting skills. And you grow your recruiting skills by growing your interpersonal skills. You start talking to people. You get people on your team who can help you recruit. You get your volunteers recruiting one or two people at a time. If you're sitting back and waiting on people to sign up to volunteer, it's not going to happen. You have to get out of your office. You have to start talking and building relationships with people and casting a vision and asking them to join your team.

No. 8: How do I get volunteers trained for special needs ministry? Now, I bring up special needs ministry as an example. Special needs ministry is one of the areas you could have the greatest impact in your community because there are so many kids and families impacted by special needs. A wrong approach is: Well, I want to start a special needs ministry. How do I get volunteers trained because there are a million different kinds of special needs and the spectrum is so large? That's the wrong question.

The right question to ask is: How do I get my church to love and accept kids and families with special needs? Because, as I mentioned in a previous chapter, love and acceptance is 80% of the volunteer's role and 20% is being trained. You need to pray for God to give you the people in your church and leadership the love and the acceptance of kids with special needs and their families.

No. 9: I wonder what would happen if I had more paid staff? Now, we all wish we had more paid staff because we feel like we could get a lot more done. But this is the wrong question to ask. If you get hung up on the fact that your church won't hire an administrative assistant or preschool director, you're going to get stuck at that obstacle.

The right question to ask is: What would happen if I got organized and learned to delegate? So much of your success in life and ministry is learning to get organized. And as a ministry leader where you oversee so many ministries and volunteers, part of getting organized is learning to delegate.

How are you doing organizationally? Are you getting done what you need to get done? Create some routines. Use a calendar. Create a to-do list. Use a productivity planner that I talked to you about in a previous chapter. Keep up with your emails. Keep your desk clean. Otherwise your eyes will drift and you'll get distracted with all kinds of stacks and notes. Keep that desk clean. Find people who can help you do things so that you can do what only you can do. Don't focus on the fact that you need more paid staff. Focus on getting organized, casting a vision, and delegating to people who can help you make the difference.

Let's end this chapter with this wrong question.

No. 10: How many kids did I have on Sunday? Granted, most churches and children's pastors track this. But it's not the right question. The right question to ask: How often do kids come? It's important to track how many, but it's more important to track frequency.

You might look back five years ago and see that some siblings cam every week. They might have missed now and then because they were sick or on vacation, but they were at church consistently. Then you go back three years ago and the same siblings were there every other week on average – twice a month. In general, twice a month became the new every week.

Now, unfortunately, families who used to go to church twice a month are now coming just once a month. Folks like Larry Fowler with the Legacy Coalition and Reggie Joiner in the Rethink Group are showing us that as they study churches, the frequency of attendance in many churches is one week out of four. That ought to frighten us as ministry leaders on many different levels. One week out of four. I mean, how do you make a deep impact if you have kids for just one hour a month? It reminds you of something essential: you have to make sure that you're equipping mom and dad to do their job as spiritual leaders all the other days of the week.

So don't just measure how many kids you had on Sunday. Measure frequency of attendance and look at what that means practically?

FINAL THOUGHT

Remember that the power of the answers you receive are directly proportionate to the kinds of questions you ask. So, if you want good solutions and to do great things, you have to learn to ask the right questions.

MY TAKEAWAYS

MY TAKEAWAYS

_____

_____

_____

_____

_____

_____

_____

_____

_____

_____

_____

_____

_____

_____

_____

_____

_____

_____

_____

_____

_____

_____

_____

MY TAKEAWAYS

NO. 7

"Lord, help me to lead even when it hurts."

NONE OF US ARE IMMUNE from pain, especially in the work of the ministry. When we work with people, we're working with kids, families, volunteers, leaders, and a congregation. One thing that comes with people is pain. A key or a secret to longevity in ministry is learning to lead through the pain.

That's why Sentence No. 7 is this: Lord, help me to lead even when it hurts.

Sam Chand, the author of *Leadership Pain*, says, "There is no growth without change, no change without loss, and no loss without pain. Bottom line: if you're not hurting, you're not leading." Sam goes on to say that leaders are bleeders, and part of leadership is managing and stewarding pain. Now, as much as leadership hurts, the good news is that pain and hurt can make you better, and they can help you grow. As a children's pastor, you're going to experience pain. As a children's ministry director, things are going to happen that are going to hurt. Let me share a few examples.

No. 1: There will be some kids in your ministry who walk away from the Lord as a teenager or a young adult.

No. 2: Some kids won't listen when you present the Gospel, and they will reject the good news of Jesus Christ.

No. 3: Some of your best volunteers will quit for one reason or another.

No. 4: Some of the spiritual leaders in your life will fall into sin. The enemy leaves no one off his radar. As a Christian leader, you have a big target on your back.

No. 5: Some parents will get mad over something seemingly insignificant and will leave the church.

No. 6: Some spiritual mentors will let you down. They may not fall into sin, but they will let you down. You have to learn to encourage yourself in the Lord as David did.

No. 7: Some significant contributions that you make to your ministry will go unnoticed. No one will say thanks. No one will acknowledge all the effort. You won't get the pat on the back you need. In fact, some will even criticize you.

No. 8: Some will lose a child to death. This is one of the most difficult things about being a children's ministry pastor or director. Helping families navigate those very difficult and gut-wrenching days after they lose a child is emotional and exhausting.

No. 9: Some people in your church just won't like you. No matter how hard you try, you won't connect with everyone.

No. 10: Some days you will feel really lonely. You will feel left out. You will feel like you don't have value.

No. 11: Some people in your church will view children's ministry as childcare.

No. 12: People who are supposed to be your close friends will let you down. It happened to Jesus, and it can happen to you.

Now, as we think about leading through pain and even when it hurts, one of the greatest passages of Scripture to encourage us is Joshua 1. In Joshua 1, Moses (the great leader of the Israelite people) died and there was a lot of pain that came along with coming to terms with his death and accepting the new leader, Joshua. There are some strategies in Joshua 1 that helped Joshua through the pain he was experiencing. I've adapted them from an article I found on pastors.com. These five strategies helped me during a difficult time in ministry, and I'm sharing them with you because I want them to help you as well.

STRATEGY NO. 1: ACKNOWLEDGE THE SITUATION

You can't ignore what's happening. Too many leaders get really good at burying their heads in the sand and trying to sweep things under the rug. But that's not leading with strength. It's a sign of weakness. God said in Joshua 1:2, "Moses my servant is dead." Now, it doesn't get much clearer than that, right? He made Joshua face the reality. There come points in our ministry where we will face a certain reality: someone lets you down, someone leaves the ministry or church, someone said something to you in public that should have been said in private. Don't ignore it or pretend like it didn't happen. Acknowledge it. Acknowledge the pain. Acknowledge what happened. You can't deal with something until you acknowledge its presence.

STRATEGY NO. 2: GET READY

God encouraged Joshua to acknowledge the situation, but not to dwell on it. That's very important to remember. Too often, leaders dwell on their hurts without recognizing and moving forward with what God has in store for them. Joshua 1:2 says, "Moses my servant is dead. Now therefore arise, go over this Jordan, you and all this people, into the land that I am giving to them, to the people of Israel." Don't miss those words, "Now therefore..." Some of you may be spending a little too much time acknowledging the pain instead of getting ready for what's next. God is writing a beautiful chapter in your life. He wants to tell a great story through you.

By the way, did you know your legacy isn't something you leave when you're dead and gone? That's only part of it. Your legacy begins today. If I recognize that my legacy begins today, that's going to impact my decisions and mindset today. Don't spent too much time dwelling on the hurts. Your pastor may have let you down. The church board may have let you down. Your best friend may have let you down. Please don't spend too much time dwelling on it. Acknowledge it and grieve. But then get ready for what's next.

STRATEGY NO. 3: REMEMBER THE PROMISE

God knows you're hurting and He wants you to know that He is always with you. In your pain, embrace His presence and protection. He will be there to help you and guide you along the way. In Joshua 1:3-5, He told Joshua, "Every place that the sole of your foot will tread upon I have given to you, just as I promised to Moses...No man shall be able to stand before you all the days of your life. Just as I was with Moses, so I will be with you. I will not leave you or forsake you."

Remember the promise God made to you. Remember the vision God gave you. Remember the calling that God has placed upon your life. He who began a good work in you will be faithful to complete it. He has begun writing a story in your life, and He is going to see that story through until the end. Acknowledge the hurt. Get ready for what's next. And remember the promise.

STRATEGY NO. 4: STAY STRONG

You need to stay strong. And while you're staying strong, you find the strength to lead. Stay strong, stay courageous, stay bold, and lead on. To lead through pain, you need to find strength and courage. Leading was not an option back in Joshua's day. He had to stay strong and lead. In Joshua 1:6, God said, "Be strong and courageous, for you shall cause this people to inherit the land that I swore to their fathers to give them." Let me encourage you to find strength. Where do you find strength? You find strength in the Lord. You find strength in Him. Don't lean on your own strength. Lean in on the Lord.

STRATEGY NO. 5: STAY IN THE WORD

Learn the gift of meditating in God's Word. This was probably the best advice that God gave Joshua, and it's found in Joshua 1:7-8. He talks about obeying the law in order to be successful and prosperous. In the Bible you hold in your hands and use to teach those kids week after week, there is a healing balm for those painful moments that come. Stay in the Book. What you do with the Word of God determines what God does with you. Make much of the Word of God. My prayer for you is that you don't view God's Word as a thick textbook, something you only crack open when you have to. But instead, I pray that you will view God's Word as a love letter written from God to you.

Remember those love letters that you used to receive back when you were dating? You opened them slowly, you smelled them, and you read them. You savored every work. And you rad them again and again. Spend time falling in love with God's Word. As you spend time in God's Word, it becomes that healing balm for your soul and spirit.

FINAL THOUGHT

God doesn't require you to have it all figured out. You're not going to know how to deal with every problem and every pain up front. What He does ask is for you to trust in Him even during the most difficult times. As pastors, we often view ourselves as the fixers, the problem solvers, the superheroes; but we need to remind ourselves that we are doing God's job. We serve an extraordinary God who can help us overcome extraordinary pain. Leading during difficult times of pain is not always easy, but with God, it is more than possible.

Today, even as I write this, I pray for those who have been impacted by deep pain. Maybe it's by a close friend, a volunteer, or your pastor. I pray that God would remind you of these five strategies from Joshua 1; remind you that although your pain is great, God is greater. I pray that the Lord will help you acknowledge your pain and then get ready for what's next; to hold on to the promises, to stay strong. and to lead while you are meditating in the Word. Together, we can pray and ask God to help us to love each other, to encourage one another, to pray for each other – all so that we can give Him the praise and the thanks.

MY TAKEAWAYS

MY TAKEAWAYS

MY TAKEAWAYS

MY TAKEAWAYS

NO. 8

"Lord, bring the right people into my life at the right time."

THIS CHAPTER WILL FOCUS ON Sentence No. 8: Lord, bring the right people into my life at the right time. A lot of pastors and ministry leaders go at it alone, but that's not God's plan. Proverbs 19:20 says, "Listen to advice and accept instruction, that you may gain wisdom in the future." You and I need people to speak into us and help us get better. Sometimes we call those mentors. Do you have a mentor? Do you have people who you have asked to help you to grow and change and improve?

All sorts of organizations use the mentoring process to help people become better at what they do. In medicine, doctors mentor young doctors. In music, musicians mentor other musicians. In athletics, athletes mentor other athletes. Why do they do this? Because it works. We work best when we have other people speaking into our lives and ministries. Whether you are new in ministry or a veteran, you need a mentor. LeBron James is one of the best basketball players on the planet, yet he needs a mentor.

One of the greatest reasons we need a mentor is because we can be blindsided by issues that, on our own, we aren't prepared to handle or we might not see as being an issue in the first place. Let me give you a few examples: managing budgets, security and safety, death of infants or children, sexual predators, special needs, toxic work cultures, problems at home, and conflicts among leadership. When we face these issues that we ourselves aren't prepared to deal with, a mentor can help us navigate them and get through them effectively.

Mentors also keep us from making dumb mistakes. I have made plenty of dumb mistakes. How about you? I often make those dumb mistakes when I do things alone. Proverbs 30:2 says, "Surely I am too stupid to be a man. I have not the understanding of a man." Do you ever feel that way? A lot of times we can make dumb mistakes, but if we have a mentor or mentors, the right people at the right time, mistakes can be avoided.

Being a children's ministry leader is not easy, and it's tougher if you don't know what you're doing. Proverbs 24:6 says, "For by wise guidance you can wage your war, and in abundance of counselors there is victory." Every children's pastor needs a mentor. No matter what stage you're at in your ministry, you need someone to coach you. Whether you're 25, 35, 55, or 75, there is someone you can learn from. Proverbs 15:22 says, "Without counsel plans fail, but with many advisers they succeed."

NO. 1: ARE YOU READY FOR A MENTOR?

You'll know you're ready based upon how you answer the following questions: Do I want to grow personally and professionally? Do I want to learn? Am I ready to listen even if I don't like what I hear? Am I ready to make some hard changes? Am I willing to put time into a mentoring relationship? Am I prepared to do the work that comes with having a mentor?

NO. 2: WHAT DO YOU LOOK FOR IN A MENTOR?

You've determined you're ready for a mentor. So, what do you look for in a mentor?

Pastor Rick Warren says this: "A mentor brings out the best in you in three areas – your roles, your goals, and your soul." A mentor is going to bring out the best in you. Now let me give you a few things to look for in a mentor.

First, find someone you want to be like. Find someone who has character, someone you admire. Proverbs 27:17 says, "Iron sharpens iron, and one man sharpens another." Find someone who you want to be like. And it doesn't have to be an Andy Stanley-type leader. I find that a lot of young leaders hold out because they want an Andy Stanley-level leader to mentor them. Well, that's not always easy or even possible, so don't look for position. Look for character when you're looking for a mentor. Who is somebody you want to be like and emulate? That's the person you need to seek out.

Second, find someone who is good at something you want to be good at. What is it you need to learn? Maybe it's how to be a better teacher, how to get organized, how to cast vision, how to walk with the Lord, how to structure your ministry for growth, how to be a better parent, how to dream bigger, how to handle your finances, how to plan for the future, how to do social networking, how to write a book. Determine what is it you want and need to learn and then find someone to help you get there. A great definition of a mentor is someone who has been where you want to go and is willing to help you get there.

Third, find someone you can open up to. There has to be a level of trust with your mentor. If you don't trust your mentor, you're not going to learn anything from him or her. Benjamin Franklin said, "Tell me and I forget. Teach me and I may remember. Involve me and I learn." In their book *As Iron Sharpens Iron*, Howard Hendricks and his son William say, "You can discover what you need in a mentor by asking yourself three questions. Number 1, what do I want my life to look like in ten years? Number 2, what will it take to achieve that? Number 3, what stands between me and that outcome?"

What do you want your life to look like in ten years? What do you want your family to look like in ten years? What will it take to achieve that? If this is what you want, what do you need to get there? What stands between where you are today and where you want to be? The gap between is what you call doing a gap analysis. This is where I am today and this is where I want to be in ten years. What stands in the gap? What's it going to take to get me from point A to point B, and who can help get me there? The answers to these questions help you decide what kind of mentor you need.

NO. 3: HOW DO YOU FIND A MENTOR?

Let's wrap up this chapter by talking through three ways to find a mentor. Howard Hendricks says to pray, look, and ask/contact. First, you need to pray. Ask God to bring the right people into your life at the right time. People who can help you grow and change and become better. Learning by having a mentor is a sign of humility, and we know that God honors humility. If you are praying for a mentor and your motives are pure in your request, I believe that God will answer your prayers. Be sensitive to God's activity in your life. Look around. Who is God bringing your way? The answers may come in places you don't expect, which leads me to the second step: look.

You have to look and be intentional. You may have mentors around you right now who you don't even see. Don't look for someone like yourself. Don't look for someone who would be expected. Look for the unexpected. That's often where the answers come.

Finally, Howard Hendricks says that if you want a mentor, you have to start asking and connect. One reason you may not have a mentor is because you haven't asked or connected. I would even encourage you not to ask someone. Instead, build a relationship. Start with a simple conversation. I have five mentors in my life. I haven't asked any of them to be my mentor. I just built a relationship and started having some conversations and have watched it develop into a mentoring relationship.

You may have someone on your heart who you think would be a great mentor but who seems really busy. Well, don't be afraid to ask because they're busy. Bill Hybels calls it making the "big ask." The big ask is asking someone who you think would never say yes. But you know what? There are a lot of people who would say yes. They just need to be asked.

FINAL THOUGHT

You and I need people speaking into our lives. 1 Corinthians 10:12 says, "Therefore let anyone who thinks that he stands take heed lest he fall." As ministry leaders, we desperately need relationships and we need to pray that God would bring the right people into our lives at the right time.

MY TAKEAWAYS

MY TAKEAWAYS

_____

_____

_____

_____

_____

_____

_____

_____

_____

_____

_____

_____

_____

_____

_____

_____

_____

_____

_____

_____

_____

_____

_____

_____

MY TAKEAWAYS

SENTENCE

NO. 9

"Lord, help me to communicate with confidence."

I N THIS CHAPTER, we'll focus on this sentence: Lord, help me communicate with confidence. Leaders are communicators. Your job day after day, week after week, month after month, and year after year is to communicate effectively. The type of communication we'll deal with specifically in this chapter is presentations: lessons, sermons, and meetings.

A question for you: Do you get nervous when you need to get up in front of a group of people to talk? If you do, know that you're in good company. I read recently that only four percent of the population feels comfortable standing up in front of a group to give a speech, sermon, etc. We know that for many people, public speaking can be stressful and create tension. It can even lead to panic and panic attacks. My prayer is that this chapter will encourage you to grow as a communicator. Good leaders are good communicators, and great leaders are great communicators.

Notice that I didn't say great leaders are great talkers. There's a big difference between talking and communicating, right? In fact, John Maxwell wrote a book titled, *Everyone*

Communicates, Few Connect. There is a lot of truth to those four words: everyone communicates, few connect.

Here's a question to consider: What is the goal of communication? Is the goal of a presentation to simply give information? Is the goal to try to get people to feel something? It ca be these, but I think it's much more than that. The goal of communication is more than just giving information – it's inspiring people to action. Communication is more than just trying to evoke feelings from people. It's leading people to do something.

If you're an effective communicator, you give your ideas handles so that others can hop on the bike and run with what you've shared. I want information to move people to act. As a children's ministry leader, you communicate all the time. More than likely, you teach kids every Sunday. You lead meetings. You give presentations. You may even preach at your church's services. Do you realize that the goal of every one of those communication opportunities is to inspire people to do something? You want those kids to hear what you're saying. You want them to understand. You want them to get it in their mind and heart. You want to lay a foundation for them, but then you want them to act.

When I'm making a presentation to a board or committee, I don't want to just communicate information. I want to lead that group to action. Now, if you choose to be an effective communicator and you pray, Lord, help me to communicate with confidence, you're going to stand apart. In fact, there are four areas where people who are excellent communicators stand apart.

NO. 1: EFFECTIVE COMMUNICATORS PRESENT WITH EXCELLENCE

If you're an effective communicator, you present with excellence. Part of presenting with excellence includes knowing your material (being prepared) and knowing your audience.

By the way, let me encourage you to strive for excellence in every area of your ministry including your communication skills.

NO. 2: EFFECTIVE COMMUNICATORS STAND APART BECAUSE THEY EXPAND THEIR PLATFORM

What's your platform? Michael Hyatt wrote an entire book called *Platform*. In the book, he talks about what a platform is and it's history. A platform was a raised stage that elevated the speaker over the audience so that everyone could hear the speaker. Platforms go back before sound systems. They were essential because they allowed the speaker to stand out above all other noise. There's a lot of noise in the world today, isn't there? And there are a lot of people trying to get everyone else's attention. If you're an effective communicator, your platform will rise. People will pay more attention to you. They will listen to what you have to say.

NO. 3: EFFECTIVE COMMUNICATORS GET MORE DONE

Do you know how they get more done? They get more done through others because they understand that the goal of a presentation is to put handles on their information so people can run with what they're saying.

NO. 4: EFFECTIVE COMMUNICATORS GROW THEIR INFLUENCE

They inspire people and move them to action. If you're going to be an effective communicator, especially in terms of public speaking, it's going to take effort to learn the art of it. But it's a skill you can develop. Maybe you don't feel like you're a natural presenter. Maybe you struggle with getting up in front of a crowd and talking. I understand that it does come easier for some than others. But growing as a communicator is a skill that you can develop and I want to help you with this.

I'm going to give you ten tips for creating powerful presentations and communicating with excellence.

TIP NO. 1: PREPARATION IS EVERYTHING

Very few people are natural presenters. There are a lot of people who are confident, but that doesn't mean they're a natural presenter. Few people can stand up in front of a microphone and have everything they want to say come naturally. So, because those people are the minority, we have to prepare.

I don't know about you, but I've found that the more prepared I am, the more confident I feel. That's why I don't like to wing it when it comes to teaching kids. Yes, there are Sundays that we have to wing it. But winging it shouldn't be the norm. Preparation is important. When I'm preaching in church, I want to prepare plenty in advance. I'll preach to myself in the car, in the mirror, and I'll even go to church when no one is there so I can practice in the sanctuary. The more prepared I am, the more confident I feel.

If you fail to prepare, you prepare to fail. This is one of the biggest mistakes that I see ministry leaders make. They have great content, they have a great heart, and they are passionate, but they don't prepare.

TIP NO. 2: YOU MUST CONNECT WITH YOUR AUDIENCE

Where there is no connection, there can be no contribution. You've probably heard someone speak before (maybe it's a pastor or a workshop or a seminar presenter) and because there's no connection within 30 seconds, that speaker becomes boring. And guess what? As a result, that speaker does not contribute to your life.

Effective communication is built on the foundation of being relational. So you have to convey a sense of relationship with your audience. In fact, it's said that you only have about 30 seconds to connect with your audience. Whether that audience is kids or adults, you have about 30 seconds to connect. I'll share some ideas on how to connect in a little bit, but right now, please know that you have to connect. If you connect, your audience will want to hear from you again and again and again.

TIP NO. 3: YOU MUST KEEP YOUR VISUALS SIMPLE

I like using slides and other visual elements when I speak, but sometimes they're a bit overrated. People aren't there to read your slides. People are there to hear from you. This is why I say keep your visuals simple. I don't want people looking at the screen all the time. When I'm teaching kids, I don't want their eyes on the screen. I want their eyes on me. So, keep your visuals simple.

TIP NO. 4: DON'T USE NOTES UNLESS YOU FREEZE

You want to talk from your notes, but you want your speaking to be more like a conversation. You don't want to have your head buried in your notes. I try to memorize what I want to say but leave room for changes on the fly. I still have the notes with me in case I freeze, but I try to create a conversation. Now, if you memorize, I do want to warn you that it's possible to come across as robotic. When you memorize your lesson/presentation, it can be a challenge to exude your passion and excitement. It's a delicate balance to find – memorizing text, but allowing your passion to flow.

How do you memorize? Some people read their notes over and over again until they can look away from the page and see the text in their head and remember it while they speak. Some write or type their main points with a couple sub-points and that's all they need.

What I like to do when preaching to large groups is to use mind maps. You might remember mind mapping from high school or college. It involves systematically drawing or writing things on a piece of paper to help you memorize or organize content. Actually, its original intent is to help people organize or systemize content, but mind maps can also be very effective when it comes to memorizing text. I first got this idea from Ed Young, Jr., at Fellowship Church.

TIP NO. 5: CREATE CONVERSATIONS

The biggest way to kill a presentation is to talk at your audience instead of talking with them. There's a big difference between "at" and "with." In the interactive, digital world we live in, people want to have a voice, so create conversations. Involve them in your presentations.

Technology creates conversations. This is why *American Idol* and *America's Got Talent* are so popular. People want to contribute and give their voice and speak into who their favorite person is. At polleverywhere.com you can create a live poll, shoot it up on the screen, ask people to text their answers, and then the screen is populated in real time with the results.

Another way to create conversations in your presentations is audience involvement. If you're teaching kids, include something in your lesson that requires an assistant.

TIP NO. 6: ASK QUESTIONS

Questions pull people in. When you ask questions, guess what? People answer. Then you have a conversation rolling.

Great communicators ask good questions. How did Jesus teach? He asked questions, right? In fact, He often answered questions with questions. Questions are a subtle tool of persuasion. In other words, if I want to move people from point A to point B, I can try to get them there by hitting them over the head with my five points, or I can ask a couple good questions and watch as they get to point B on their own. Questions are also a good way to get feedback. It helps you understand if your audience really gets it before it's too late. You can ask questions and have people raise their hand. You can also ask questions and ask people to respond verbally. When you ask questions and invite feedback, it helps to keep your audience's attention.

How many of you remember screen savers? We don't use them as much these days. After a certain number of minutes passed, the screen saver appears. And to get that screen saver to go away, you have to move the mouse or press a key. People have built-in screen savers. After a while, your audience's screen savers will appear if you don't engage and connect. One of the best ways to get that screen saver to either never start or to go away is to ask great questions. Great questions pull people in.

TIP NO. 7: USE PROPS

Effective communicators use props. Think of all the props and object lessons God used to communicate throughout the Bible. Think of the rainbow and Noah's ark. Think of Jesus when He taught about the needle in the haystack, the camel going through the eye of the needle, the lost coin, and the lost sheep.

Object lessons have been around for a long time. You now why? Because they work! And not only with kids, but also with adults. When you do an object lesson, you're taking a concrete physical object and connect it to an abstract spiritual truth. People connect with that object, and they resonate with it and relate it to a spiritual truth.

By the way, handouts don't count as an object lesson or props. If you're reading this book, more than likely you work with kids. There are so many kinds of props you can use with kids! You can use everyday household objects. Do a search on the Internet and you can find virtually countless ideas for object lessons. You can do magic tricks or illusions. You can use slides. You can use video clips. You can put something in their hands. It can be a craft. It can be a hands-on activity. When you use props and objects, the sudden the retention level of those you are communicating to rises.

TIP NO. 8: TELL STORIES

Effective communicators tell stories. In general, people tend to be persuaded more by stories than by facts and figures. That's why we get bored when people start talking about statistics and economics. But when stories are included in the presentation, we connect and are more persuaded. Jesus was a master story-teller. He told all kinds of stories as part of his teaching. Stories are effective and they're not just effective for kids.

TIP NO. 9: REMOVE PHYSICAL BARRIERS

I almost hesitated to include this point because I don't know if it's for everyone. But I have always had a hard time with stages and lecterns and pulpits. It's probably because I'm a kid guy, and I'm always moving among the kids to keep their attention. So, for me, it helps to communicate and connect with the audience if I remove those barriers, whether it's a stage or a pulpit or even a desk. When I'm talking one-on-one with someone in my office, I don't like sitting across the desk. I want to be next to someone with no physical barriers between us. So, this may or may not be for you. I know pastors who are great communicators who stand behind a pulpit and don't move much.

TIP NO. 10: HAVE A CALL TO ACTION

If the point of communication is to lead people to action, you need to communicate what you want the audience to do. I read that 75% of people who leave a presentation leave without knowing the main point. That's staggering. It's essential to make it easy for people to respond. Make the call to action very clear. For example, tell them what you think they need to do tomorrow, next week, next month, etc.

FINAL THOUGHT

Overall, after you prepare and present, don't forget the power of review. Reviewing your main points with the audience is a great teaching tool. If you don't review the main points, you leave what I call a "chunk of wow" on the table. If you really want to wow your audience, review because it will help the message to stick. The key to communication, according to Jack Welch, is simplicity, consistency, and repetition.

MY TAKEAWAYS

MY TAKEAWAYS

_____

_____

_____

_____

_____

_____

_____

_____

_____

_____

_____

_____

_____

_____

_____

_____

_____

_____

_____

_____

_____

_____

MY TAKEAWAYS

_____
_____
_____
_____
_____
_____
_____
_____
_____
_____
_____
_____
_____
_____
_____
_____
_____
_____
_____
_____
_____
_____

MY TAKEAWAYS

SENTENCE

NO. 10

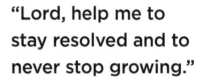

"Lord, help me to stay resolved and to never stop growing."

T HE FINAL SENTENCE that can revolutionize your ministry is: Lord, help me stay resolved and to keep growing. Here's the thing about ministry: it can be an emotional roller coaster. I see you nodding your head. There are highs and lows. Think about Elijah. Think of all the emotional roller coasters he went through. He was fed by ravens and he drank out of a river. And then he raised a boy from the dead. Then there's Mount Carmel, the battle against the prophets of Baal, and running for his life from Queen Jezebel. Talk about ups and downs.

This is how it goes in ministry, especially in children's ministry. One day you feel like you're on top of the world, and the next day you feel like you want to escape into a deep cave.

In my research, I have found that the average tenure of a children's pastor is 18 to 20 months. Now, I don't know about you, but I don't want to be that statistic. So, I'm going to share five practices that can help you stay healthy and resolved in children's ministry.

NO. 1: KEEP YOUR SPIRITUAL HEALTH A PRIORITY

Unfortunately, children's pastors and ministry leaders are busy serving God so they let their spiritual health be moved to the back burner. It's no longer a priority to them because everything in their job is urgent. One of the most important things children's pastors can do to be spiritually healthy is to make their relationship with God a priority.

There are three choices you have to make. First, you have to choose to love God more than you love your ministry. Every heart has a throne. Who is sitting on the throne of your heart? Is it the Lord, or is it your ministry? If I want to know what sits in the heart of your throne, all I have to do is follow your time, your money, your thoughts, and your priorities. Be careful that you don't fall in love with the ministry of the Lord more than you are in love with the Lord of the ministry.

The second choice is whether you will spend time with God every day in prayer. Every day. A common casualty of ministry life is one's time with the Lord. The more you talk with someone, the more you love him or her, right? Think back to when you were dating your spouse – you wanted to spend as much time as possible together and you could talk for hours and hours. So, how do you fall more and more in love with the Lord? You spend time with Him in prayer.

The third choice (which coincides with the second choice) is that you must choose to spend time in God's Word. Preparing a lesson for Sunday doesn't count. Spending time in God's Word cannot be related to your work. You need to be in the Word for your own study and enrichment – so you can hear from God as it pertains to your life.

NO. 2: JOIN A SMALL GROUP AND BE PART OF THE CHURCH COMMUNITY

Proverbs 27:17 says, "Iron sharpens iron, and one man sharpens another." Children's pastors have to be a part of the community in their local church. You have to be connected. Children's pastors and pastors in general can be some of the most well-known yet most lonely people on the planet.

Do you have people in your life providing accountability? Who is your Paul? You need a Paul. You need a small group. You need people providing you with accountability. Billy Graham once said, "I wouldn't have made it alone." We need people teaching us how to pray like Jesus taught his disciples to pray. We need people teaching us how to lead like Jesus would have us to lead.

Do you attend worship services on a regular basis? Or are you with the kids every week? While being in your church's main service is not the same as being in a small group, it's not healthy for you emotionally and spiritually to not be in the service in a regular basis. You need to build a team so that you can go into adult worship. You have a phone – you can be texted if there is an emergency. You can wear an earbud connected to your ministry's walkie-talkie system. You need to figure out a way to be in service so you can connect with your church body.

You also need to have friends outside church. If you only have friends inside your church, there is always a dual relationship. You don't want to disclose. You also don't want to over-disclose. So how do you walk the tightrope and how do you balance this dual relationship if all your friends are from your church? So, have friends who you live with and who you serve, but find some friends you can talk to about anything (which is not always possible inside the church). Sometimes it's easier to be more vulnerable with friends outside your church than people within your church.

NO. 3: LEARN TO THINK LIKE A LEADER

Jim Wideman says that the difference between leaders and followers is the way they think. Are leaders created or are they born? That's a million-dollar question, right? Here's what I found in my research: the answer is that they are both created and born. Some people are just natural-born leaders out of the womb and others grow and develop the skill. I don't have scientific data for this but I believe it's 30% genetic and 70%

learned. My conclusion comes from 20 years of working with leaders. I found that 30% of people are strong leaders because of genetics. Seventy percent of them learn to think and act like a leader. Now, it is possible for you to change the way you think. I want to encourage you to think like the leader God has created you to be. John Maxwell in his book *How Successful People Think* shares some skills of good thinkers. Let me share some of them with you.

First, John Maxwell says that good thinkers think big – they think about the big picture. They think beyond themselves and beyond their world and current realities. And good thinkers don't just think big picture; they're focused. They have a great ability to remove the clutter and distractions. They think creatively and outside the box. In fact, sometimes they don't even know there is a box. They love to explore ideas and options.

Second, good thinkers think realistically. They want to deal with the facts.

Third, good thinkers benefit from shared thinking. They search the minds of others because they understand the power that follows. They question popular thinking. They reject common thinking to get uncommon results.

NO. 4: CHOOSE TO PARTNER WITH YOUR PASTOR

According to Sam Chand, this is one of the secrets of longevity in ministry. If there is a disconnect between you and your pastor, there's a good chance you're not going to be at your church very long. Or you might be there, but you're not going to "be there" if you know what I mean.

So, avoid the problem by choosing to partner with your pastor. I'm sure there are times you wish you could vote your pastor off the island, but guess what? There have been times he has wanted to vote you off the island, too! Instead of competing with your pastor, instead of there being tension, learn to work as a team. Be his advocate the way you want him to be your advocate.

One of the greatest people who I've ever heard teach on this is my friend Brian Dollar from High Voltage Kids. In fact, I taught on this very topic with Brian at a conference. Brian has a great relationship with his pastor from First Assembly of God in North Little Rock. I've never quite seen a children's pastor and a senior pastor work together so effectively. Brian shares several secrets, and I'm going to share some of these with you to help you move from just surviving to thriving in your relationship with your pastor.

First, don't let your pastor be caught off guard. If there is a crisis or an emergency or someone is upset, let your pastor know. Don't let your pastor get caught by surprise when someone emails or calls him about the situation. Keep your pastor in the loop. Now, that doesn't mean your pastor has to be kept in the loop of the minute-to-minute details and minutia. But you know what kind of things your pastor wants to know about in advance.

Second, stay in tune with your pastor's vision and leadership. This is hard when you're with the kids week after week because pastors often share their vision from the pulpit on Sundays. If you're not in the service, y you run the chance of missing on hearing the heart of your pastor. Be in the service and for the times you can't, listen to the sermon later.

Third, avoid tunnel vision. Remember, your pastor sees the entire ministry – the kids, the teenagers, the adults, the senior adults, the outreach, what's happening now, what's happening next month, and what's happening a year from now.

Fourth, serve your pastor first. You are an assistant to your pastor first and foremost. So, before you do what you want to do, make sure you're serving your pastor, even in very practical ways. Set up his classroom for Wednesday night, run an errand for him, offer to pick up lunch for him. And, a really important way to serve your pastor is to pray for and with him.

Fifth, don't get overly attached to your job description. If your pastor needs you to teach the senior adults for two weeks, are you going to tell him no because it's not in your job description? You need to be willing to do it. If your pastor decides that the church is going to add a service on Saturday night this week, you dive in with a good attitude and help. Be willing to do anything.

Sixth, listen between the lines. Don't require direct instruction. Brian Dollar does a great job teaching this point: understand what your pastor wants, even if he doesn't ask you for it directly. Your pastor may not tell you that he wants you to wear a tie to the funeral, your pastor may not tell you that he wants the van to get cleaned after you come back from taking the kids to a water park, but listen between the lines.

Seventh, know the learning style or the love language of your pastor. Know the learning style or love language of your pastor. Don't expect your pastor to have the same learning style as you. Don't expect your pastor to have the same love language as you. Don't expect your pastor to show appreciation the same way you do.

Eighth, don't be defensive. If your pastor questions you about something, be open to listening to what your pastor is saying. Remember that he may be questioning you, but that doesn't mean he is attacking your character or questioning your motives. So, don't be defensive. Be open to input, critique, and correction.

Ninth, speak positively about your pastor. Never criticize your pastor publicly. Keep your frustrations quiet. If someone comes to you wanting to talk negatively about your pastor, defer the conversation. Don't go there.

Finally, don't allow yourself to start thinking things would be better if you were in charge. You know what?

You're not in charge, and God has called your pastor to lead. It's easy to play armchair quarterback. It's another thing to be sitting where you pastor sits.

NO. 5: CHOOSE TO TAKE CARE OF YOURSELF

You're the only you that you have. You're the only you that your spouse has. You're the only you that your children have. You're the only you that your church has, that your pastor has, that the kids in your ministry has. You have to choose to take care of yourself. Don't overwork. You are not called to work harder than your creator. Take some time off. In Mark 6:31 Jesus said, "Come away by yourselves to a desolate place and rest a while." If you don't rest, you will come apart at some point.

Get the rest you need. Too many pastors and ministry leaders go full steam for years only to look back one day with regret. We addressed this earlier in this book, but the average person needs eight or nine hours of sleep a night. If you sleep good today, that means you'll be more productive tomorrow. And focus on getting consistent good sleep, not just a night here or there.

Choose a hobby outside of work. In other words, get a life! Your life shouldn't just revolve around the church. I like woodworking. I like to travel. Beth and I like to cook. We like to spend time together in the kitchen. Find some hobbies. Don't think of these hobbies as an expense. Think of them as an investment. An investment in yourself.

In Philippians 3:12-13, Paul said this: "Not that I have already obtained this or am already perfect, but I press on to make it my own, because Christ Jesus has made me his own. Brothers, I do not consider that I have made it my own. But one thing I do: forgetting what lies behind and straining forward to what lies ahead." Paul knew he wasn't perfect. He hadn't learned everything he could learn. He knew he wasn't what he should have been. And here he was at the end of his life writing in a Philippian jail. If the apostle Paul knew that he needed to continue growing, you and I need to continue growing.

FINAL THOUGHT

Effective leaders are growing leaders. You need to stay resolved. You need to stay committed to a growth mindset. And you know what? I believe that because you've read this book, you're committed to that. So keep it up.

MY TAKEAWAYS

MY TAKEAWAYS

MY TAKEAWAYS

MY TAKEAWAYS

ABOUT THE AUTHOR

Ryan Frank is a pastor, publisher and an entrepreneur. He serves as the CEO of KidzMatter. Ryan and his wife, Beth, are the publishers of KidzMatter Magazine. He is also the co-founder of Kidmin Academy and Kidmin Nation Mega Con, the largest children's ministry conference in America. He is the author of 9 Things They Didn't Teach Me in College About Children's Ministry (Standard) Pulse (KidzMatter), Pulse 2 (KidzMatter), Give Me Jesus (Baker), and The Volunteer Code (The Leverage Group).

Ryan entered full-time ministry in 1998 after graduating from Indiana Wesleyan University with a degree in Christian Education. He was hired as children's pastor at Liberty Baptist Church where he served as Children's Pastor from 1998-2010. He was awarded a Master of Arts in Bible Exposition from Pensacola Theological Seminary in 2000.

In 1999 Ryan married Beth Bishir. Today they have three daughters. The Franks reside in Converse, Indiana.

KidzMatter was created in 2004 and is located in Marion, Indiana. The marvel is that every day KidzMatter has the opportunity, on a global scale, to shape the way people think about children's and family ministry. The fact that our resources, our magazine, our events, and website put us within reach of virtually everyone on the planet is staggering. We have a strategic opportunity to equip churches to reach children for the Lord Jesus Christ. Our passion is to provide resources that God can best use to that end.

Ryan enjoys reading, traveling and being in the backyard. You can connect with Ryan at www.KidzMatter.com or in the I Love Kidmin Facebook Group.